AF292524

Understanding WW2

Also by Andrew Sangster and in print with Pen & Sword Books

'Pug' – Churchill's Chief of Staff (2023)

How Hitler Evolved the Traditional Army Establishment
(with Pier Paolo Battistelli) (2024)

Hitler's New Command Structure and the Road to Defeat
(with Pier Paolo Battistelli) (2024)

Major Blunders of the Second World War (2024)

'Make Germany Great Again' (2024)

From Stalingrad to Italy – Von Senger's War (2025)

Exploring Nationalism (2025)

Why Appeasement Failed (2025)

Stalin's Secret Services (2026)

Dr Joseph Goebbels (2026)

Understanding WW2

Why First-hand Accounts Are So Important

Andrew Sangster

Pen & Sword
MILITARY

First published in Great Britain in 2026 by
Pen & Sword Military
An imprint of Pen & Sword Books Limited
Yorkshire – Philadelphia

ISBN 978 1 03619 413 0

A CIP catalogue record for this book is
available from the British Library.

Typeset by Mac Style
Printed in the UK by CPI Group (UK) Ltd, Croydon, CR0 4YY.

The Publisher's authorised representative in the EU for product
safety is Authorised Rep Compliance Ltd., Ground Floor,
71 Lower Baggot Street, Dublin D02 P593, Ireland.
www.arccompliance.com

For a complete list of Pen & Sword titles please contact:

PEN & SWORD BOOKS LIMITED
47 Church Street, Barnsley, South Yorkshire, S70 2AS, England
E-mail: enquiries@pen-and-sword.co.uk
Website: www.pen-and-sword.co.uk
or
PEN AND SWORD BOOKS
1950 Lawrence Road, Havertown, PA 19083, USA
E-mail: uspen-and-sword@casematepublishers.com
Website: www.penandswordbooks.com

Contents

In Defence of History

The study of history is as critically important as a geographical map for anyone negotiating a new and bewildering landscape. This is not necessarily because history repeats itself or is cyclic, but humankind, despite technological and scientific advances, remains very similar in habit to even his most ancient predecessors and appears unteachable. The modern man proud to be seen with his new expensive car is no different from his ancestors with their acquisition of a new horse, and the need to be regarded as someone of importance in his grand abode and work in life. Humankind is known to come in wide-ranging variations, some kind and helpful, others wanting to be left alone to work their way through life as comfortably as possible. There are always those who can feel they are for one reason or another important and seek status, wealth, and power, believing they are called to leadership. There may be those who sincerely believe they can improve the way we live, but others who seek power for their own egotistical reasons and can be all too determined and even ruthless to forge ahead. The study of history is basically a record of human behaviour in motivations, intentions, and actions. The sense of human progress can be detected, but also the repetition of what may be termed retrogressive behaviour, seeking power and wealth at any cost, a feature which can be found ranging from everyday criminals to would-be leaders of nations. The accounts of history are marked with traffic signals of red, green and amber warning lights. This aspect of history means this subject should not be neglected.

History books have different formats, some offering a wide approach offering a history of a country or even a continent over 2,000 years, others concentrating on particular aspects such as a civil or international war, major changes such as the Reformation, political changes of substance in the way we are governed, and some concentrating on a single person or a singular important event. The better history books carry footnotes to explain a detail, and more importantly endnotes to indicate from where the historian gained his information or viewpoint.

History can be biased when it should be objective, and some historians are well-known for being driven by nationalistic impulse, others driven by a political or religious bias, and the various driving themes behind written history can be manifold. The astute reader of history will need to know the veracity of what has been written, which in terms of past centuries must rely on such studies as archaeology, national boundaries, preserved documents, and any surviving views expressed at the time in question, be it ancient documents or artifacts. It is about going back in time to collect reliable evidence.

In terms of modern history relating to the twentieth century, which was important, because it was a century of war, including two world wars and tainted with the fear of global annihilation which persists to this day, the historian is able to draw on various forms of Oral History with evidence from people who were there, some in leadership roles, many who were involved in momentous events, and more from those who observed, suffered at home or on the battlefields. Today, given the time span since 1945, Oral History is mainly dependent on archives and published works based on these sources. To open up the vast experience of such works, many are mentioned, the personal source described as the most reliable, and a few extracts are provided to give a taste of the nature of the work. Some deserve more space than others, but they all open what may be called 'inside knowledge'.

This kind of evidence not only adds to every form of historical work, but makes the reading of history more interesting.

Foreword

The hieroglyphics cut into ancient monuments some 2,000 to 3,000 years ago are always studied for any information about who was leading, the nature of the times and so forth. Even Biblical scholars still study ancient papyrus documents to determine the earliest by numbering them, P45 and so forth. The critical Christian gospels have been studied, with scholars establishing St Mark was the earliest gospel to be written followed by St Matthew and St Luke's Gospel using parts which became known as the Synoptic problem, and St John's Gospel the last to be written. It was not undervaluing the last written gospel but naturally felt the earliest one was important for historical reasons. This is not what many people would call Oral History but the written word close to the events under study is the next best thing, and this remains true today. A person writing down the events as they witnessed them is a critical element in finding the best sources for historical research. There are sometimes doubts that the truth is being evaded for a variety of reasons, which is when it is over to the historian to accept or question the material, and the general reader to make his or her judgment based on common sense, the evaluation of the person writing, and to question if there were hidden agendas.

Such evidence in terms of recent history can be found in many archives across the world, some easier to access than others. Archival research can be an exhausting and expensive way of study. This author can recall travelling to London in order to penetrate the shelves of the National Archives in Kew Gardens, spent days there, when obliging staff had issued an entry permit and ensured their visitor would not take or mark any documents. They then rushed around bringing the requested papers, letters, telegrams, and after nearly a week of working under a spotlight there were only two pieces of information which proved useful for the study. Today it is slightly easier because some archives are possible to search via cyber space, but one still has to be dedicated to such research.

This study came about following discussion with other historians who were seeking information about the past, not only the facts, but the feelings and emotions of the era in question. We all understood that letters, diaries, notes of meetings, even recorded interviews and committee notes could be changed to suit the writer, but it was also pointed out much valuable and reliable material has been published and can be found on the bookshelves. There are books which have studied taped recordings of conversations and interviews, committee notes, diaries and letters which are private and personal and some formal. Diaries and letters written by leading men or their servants can be revealing, as can the diaries of ordinary men and women, as they tell us much about the working of the inner circles, and often about the personalities of some top men, as well as their emotions and thoughts.

There is one major warning arising from letters, diaries, and even committee meetings that we must recall that often we are hearing or listening to opinions, not necessarily the facts. One colleague claimed it was possible to write a war history from some diaries, but it would be essential to ignore many of the personal opinions, and this warning is often made clear in Colville's diary of 10 Downing Street (reviewed later), when he decided an incident in 1940 Belgium was a 'put-up job' by the Germans when it was quite the opposite. However, this factor serves to demonstrate the confused times in which they lived, and a historian although using Oral History to understand the nature and feelings of the day needs the benefit of hindsight for later known facts. These areas are an interesting form of Oral History, but there is, just one short step away, the question of reflective memory, sometimes called the heritage of memory.

When men and women write about their memories after the events, they can still be valuable. Not everyone has time to write down their accounts, and often it is when looking back they wished they had tried. This writer's father was a fireman in the London blitz, and when asked by his impertinent son why he did not keep a diary, the reply made sense, that most of his waking hours were work, and as soon as possible they all fell asleep, to be woken for the next emergency. Reflective memory has to be treated with caution, because there are many reasons why memory can be distorted with various motives, and sometimes even a short period of time can change the impact of memory. Nevertheless, they were there, and their emotions and feelings of the day add to the interest of history. It is up to the reader to evaluate whether the truth is being told but there are even a few autobiographies which can be not only interesting but valuable for understanding the past.

This book is about the importance or Oral History and reflective memories which can be found by looking on bookshelves for material which describes the past and the emotions and feelings of the day.

Introduction

In studying the history, stories, legends before humankind developed the skill of writing, information was passed on by word of mouth. This has been called oral tradition and often used to explain stories and accounts maintained long before writing, and it often relates to the study of the early books of the Old Testament. It is somewhat different from Oral History which tends to relate more to information gathered at the time of events or immediately afterwards. The inference is not that the spoken word is necessarily retained, which thanks to developing technology some material has been, but that it was written down at the time of events, and has remained unchanged, reflecting the writer's views at the time. Oral History can include original notes of meetings, letters, unchanged diaries, and many other works which are personal to the writer. Oral History can be found in archives and published works, because such material has been recorded on tape and transcribed through keeping the events of the day in written works and in recording archives, much of such recordings can be found in the Imperial War Museum. Even local diaries kept by a family member have their own context as they can relate the feelings and emotions of the day in any city, town, or rural area. One which has recently arrived on the local bookshelves is the recorded diary of a young and intelligent schoolgirl in 1941 Norfolk, entitled *A Norfolk Girl's Home Front* (edited by Una Watson). It includes the emotions of the day, not only at family level but in wider circles. The effects of bombing, refugees, the fears for the future, and what people thought about the news on the radio and read in the newspapers. This local diary of 1941 brings home the reality of that year in that particular area.

In this light, Oral History is valuable more often than not in understanding not only what happened but the feelings and emotions of the day. There are various historical accounts of ancient and medieval battles, sometimes even in tapestry, but imagine how much more would have been gleaned from a diary or letters home to the family from the soldiers and their leaders.* Imagine, at the stretch of the imagination being able to talk to one of these fighters and able to discuss precisely what happened, their own thoughts on the reasons for the battle, and how they felt. This needs imagination, but today we can talk to someone of our previous generation or even the one behind that. This writer is old enough to recall being fascinated listening to his parents talk about the Second World War and one grandparent in-law who fought in the First World War, and speaking to a man who limped because of a parachute misadventure at the Battle of Arnhem. It was these early youth discussions with a generation who were part of his life which implanted a life-long obsession with history. It happened because hearing the accounts of people who were there, who had no axe to grind, brought a reality to the school textbooks.

Today Oral History is slowly being recognised as valuable in understanding the past, and it has become a subject of interest and study in all occupations. We hear of some communities or business organisations burying time capsules, and books written by all types of modern organisations using various means of conveying the lessons from the past to the future.[1] In a court of law the most important evidence is that produced by an eyewitness, by camera, by film and recording, and hearsay evidence is rejected. The courtroom demands total truth from an eyewitness, no forged or bigoted evidence, not hearsay, just the known ascertainable truth. For the same reason, films, photos, and recorded interviews from the past are taken seriously by students of

---

* The Bayeux Tapestry is a 230 foot long and 20-inch-tall work which depicts events leading up to the Norman conquest of England in 1066. It is thought to date to the eleventh century, a few years after the battle.

history. More recently the legal professionals have to check there is no AI or computer technology in use, but that is a very recent issue.

In the imagined scenario of talking to ancient or medieval combatants, the archer and swordsman might be able to express the conditions of the battle, but it would be necessary to talk with a higher commander for the reasons and the political ramifications for the battle in the first place. As this is being written in 2025 there are very few people alive who fought in the Second World War, and in March 2025 the news announced the death of the last British fighter-pilot from that period. Even those born at the end of the war in 1945 are now 80 years of age. However, by the nineteenth-twentieth centuries writing and reading was, except for a very few, in widespread use. Despite the fact that the written word is not necessarily oral, it is nearly as good as an acceptable form of communication, especially if it can be verified that it was written at the time with no hidden agenda.

Reflective History, or the Heritage of Memory

There are variations of reliability in recorded Oral History which must always be kept in mind. Letters, notes, diaries which were written at the time of events are probably the most reliable source of sound information. By the use of this word information, it does not mean just ascertaining the facts and events of the day, but the feelings, reactions, and emotions of those involved. That which is recalled later needs greater scrutiny, sometimes referred to as the heritage of memory. Reflective memories can change as the months and years pass. This does not mean that they should be disregarded, but they should be treated with caution and carefully weighed in the balance of reliability.

Oral History always needs close scrutiny, written works and even taped recordings can be changed for personal or political reasons. There are many possible explanations why memories either change as their 'shades of recounting' can be diminished or exaggerated. Some memories are enhanced or reduced for personal reasons, and sometimes the account is changed out of embarrassment, or thinking the account is too terrible to relate and may be moderated. These factors have to be considered when reading even the most honest accounts and even hearing personal conversations. This does not make them worthless, because the various reasons for changes can be of historical interest as to why alterations may have been made. This applies to any form of Oral History, and also to what may be called reflective memory or the heritage of memory when past events are recalled by a participant even in the recent past. Using Oral History or reflective memory often has to be counterbalanced or scrutinised by known historical facts.

Nevertheless, when heard or read, this aspect of 'memory' directly offers valuable historical insights, not least because the listener can judge whether the conveyor of the account is a person who is not prone to exaggeration or seeking either glory or justification for his or her actions, or even some hidden political agenda. Most of the insights explored do not reflect on the overall strategies of a war though some do, but they convey the feelings of the person, and some outline the background to past events which can be critical. The first chapter will recall this writer's experience after talking to such people over a period of sixty plus years. This is termed 'oral history' but written accounts reflecting this can be just as good if they are judged to be honest accounts. This study will explore some publications which use Oral History as their main basis and try and evaluate their usefulness and integrity.

Oral History of the twentieth century World Wars was a dominant feature for young people in the 1950s as the bombsites were a feature of many cities, ports and some towns. Today the World Wars of the twentieth century have started to fade as somewhat remote in distant history, almost irrelevant. When Oral History comes to light, especially at the personal level, it captures the past offering a sense of past times, not only enlivening history, but opens the vista and warnings of times which could be repeated. Normal history books can be seen by some as too clinical and belonging to academia, which is unfair but for some all too true, but reliable Oral History gives a sense of the immediacy of experience and disaster. Remembered or recorded conversations can offer intriguing insights into the realities of the past. This writer has decided to start this study with his own experience of listening to previous generations, but many books have also been written on the subject, not just with dealing with the Second World War but life in the 1930s, one of the more interesting compiled by Peter Liddle, *Captured Memories*.[2] Nevertheless, it must be recalled that they reflect the emotions of the past, and although this is invaluable and often intriguing, they remain, although significant, a cautious area of Oral History, as will be explored in Chapter One.

In terms of reflective memory, it is occasionally possible to read autobiographies which clearly show they have pulled no punches, not enhanced themselves, and told the truth not only of what happened, but what they thought at the time, and sometimes admitting they thought differently postwar. These publications fall under the category of Reflective Oral History, or the Heritage of Memory. There are very few of these reflective memories which come close to Oral History, but some have been selected because by their author's writing the clear truthfulness can be supported from other sources. It could be claimed that these belong more to what one may call reminiscent history, but a reader of history should be able to pick up when reading a reflection which is being honestly recalled. One of the lesser-known ones was an autobiographical account of a teenage spitfire pilot who admitted he was scared, panicked, was not always efficient, and admitted he kept copious notes of his feelings by his bed. This book will be explored in the chapter relating to autobiographies.

This is vastly different from biographies unless they have letters from the subject or genuine diary insertions. Many biographies become hagiographies, but the better ones try and paint an honest picture, but they only become of historical interest if they have evidence of the subject's private thinking through letters and diary notes. There is always the danger that many autobiographies are compiled as apologias, even self-justification, or even personal glory, but this study explores five examples which feel as if they could have been written as the related events unfold.

Oral History

Oral History can still be found in its 'purest state' when a person's feelings or perceptions or events are written down or recorded at the time and preserved unchanged. Such works are important to understanding the past and can be found in many archives. Many years ago, this writer while researching in the Kew National Archives, came across some governmental papers with Churchill's scribbled notes in the margins. The way Churchill expressed his feelings in these notes was revealing, and his strands of thought were enlightening. Sadly, Churchill was not the focus of the research at the time, and they were placed back in their folders, and left on the desk to be returned to their shelves.

Such pieces of information written at the time, often on the same day, are as good as any form of oral history because of the time factor. These written or recorded works which survive can convey the feelings and events of the day. This book focuses on those works which have been published and are easily accessible, as searching through archives takes time and money to travel, can be exhausting, time consuming, and often fruitless.

Letters home to loved ones would not pass the censor if they gave away information, but they often illustrated the feelings of the day and conveyed a broad picture of the circumstances. When this writer was visiting a British Legion Home for war veterans of the First World War, in Aylesford in Kent in 1969, he read a letter from the widow's husband sent in 1916. It was difficult to read as it was written in pencil on faded paper the size of a toilet sheet. The husband explained it might be his last letter, as he wanted his wife to know he loved her. The previous day he had been ordered to cross a minefield while under fire, there were five of them and he was the only survivor. He noted that he was so scared he was glad to be wearing khaki because he lost control of his bowels, though he expressed it in a slightly more basic way. He had shot a German soldier and said he wondered why, because he looked just like his Uncle John, adding words like 'I have no idea what this bloody war is about'. In a strange way this one-page letter brought the feelings of many in the trenches home. He survived and died in 1969 when this writer as a young priest took his funeral. Finding such letters in the archives can be testing, but in the chapter dealing with letters there are some from the Russian front of the Second World War, which are gripping in so far that they not only provide the battlefield circumstances, but the emotions of the day. There are also personal letters from a Nazi leader and from a German and an American military commander.

There were many who kept diaries, some cannot be trusted because they were occasionally written or later changed, but others wrote them on a weekly if not daily basis. Some used these diary entries to compile their autobiographies, others kept them intact, and as such some diaries become a source of oral history, or 'primary sources'. One example to be explored in the chapter dealing with diaries is that of Field Marshal Alan Brooke, Chief of the Imperial General Staff, whose views on Churchill are at times almost damning, even though he liked and respected the prime minister. Unlike those from the frontline, Alan Brooke's diary exposes the tussles and emotions in the top headquarters, reminding us that whether frontline soldier or sitting behind a desk we are all very human. The study also explores diaries by an Italian Foreign Minister, a Nazi politician, a German military Judge, a German diplomat, a White Russian, and a surviving German Jew, and private secretaries to the British monarchy and 10 Downing Street.

Written notes taken at the time can often be an invaluable source, many of which can be found in various archives and family lofts. One area of interest is the published works which contain notes of interrogations of the captured enemy prisoners, and many books have been written about the major Nuremberg Trial which reveal a great deal about all levels of prisoners who were questioned immediately postwar, interviewed by psychologists and psychiatrists and observed by many others. Even more interesting are some recordings taken of senior German officers held in prison camps, when they discussed the war, the strategy and the politics of the day and did so openly not realising they were being listened to over concealed bugs.

Chapter One

Oral and Reflective History

INTRODUCTION

This chapter starts by the writer recalling his own personal experience of listening to people in the postwar years recount their experiences. From about the early 1950s through to the next century out of sheer curiosity he talked to people about their experiences in the war, a juvenile occupation which grew into genuine historical interest. As he matured, he found that having some knowledge of the speaker's personality he could estimate whether the speaker was prone to exaggeration or not. By the time he became a professional historian the validity of published oral evidence or reminiscent memory had to go under the same test and be checked out as far as possible by testing the facts.

The next part of the chapter is given to those published works where historians, by digging in the archives or meeting with those involved, have produced books which often announce they are Oral History, and often deploy the use of the word 'voice' in their title, such as lost voices, or forgotten voices, and there are myriads of such titles. This chapter explores such books dipping into them to 'whet the appetite', and asking how far they can be reliable, which most are.

PERSONAL TO THIS WRITER

Author's Note: *The first part of this chapter will be in the first person as it relates to my personal experience of talking directly to people of earlier generations, which generated my love of history.*

In 1954-5 as a nine to ten-year old boy brought up in Dover, Kent, I used to find excitement with a couple of friends by penetrating the tunnels under Dover Castle which had once been a military headquarters, now famous for visitors as it had been Admiral Ramsay's headquarters during the Dunkirk retreat. When we found our way in by using a stolen skeleton key from a sentry box, we found with our torches much material still in place.* Some typewriters were on the desks, some clothes still on the pegs, nothing too exciting. I pocketed two items, a mortar bomb, and a hand-grenade. At home I decided to bury the bomb in the back garden and hid the hand-grenade in the shed. I went out for a game of football in the street as there were few cars in those days. I was surprised when a khaki-coloured van drove up outside and three men rushed into my neighbour's house. To cut a long story short, my neighbour, a retired rear admiral had watched me bury the mortar-bomb and called them in for help. I was summoned by my mother as they dug up that part of the garden and I was given a sound telling off, but the neighbour asked that the police be kept out of the scene, and his rank saved my skin. The next day I was sent by my parents to apologise to my naval neighbour, and this started a long relationship during which this kind old man told me much of his life as a serving officer in the Royal Navy during the First World War. Sadly, I never kept notes, but I recall him telling me that when his naval vessel was on patrol, he was all too aware that they were a significant target as they were alone without planes in the vast

---

* This 'skeleton key' stayed in my possession for many years, it opened the front door of my girlfriend's house, and many years later when teaching at Eton School it opened doors there.

stretches of the sea and worried about the unseen enemy of U-boats. He recalled the times he was often on the ship's bridge searching the horizon for hostile ships or signs of a periscope, and explained he was quite deaf because naval guns were noisy and difficult to avoid. I can recall two features of this man and his memories: the tears in his eyes when speaking of a friend killed in action, and his sense of fear when on patrol. He died a few years later but left me as a mere boy with the impression that war had to be avoided when possible, and it was not a 'glorious adventure'. I also promised myself I would never join the navy as it was always a lonely target for the enemy. I still have in my library an atlas he gave me.

He had inadvertently made me interested in history As a teenager I managed to encourage my father to talk of his time as a London fireman in the blitz, recalling his fear on going up a ladder with a high-powered fire hose, and wondering whether his weight at that height would overturn the seemingly small vehicle below controlling and holding the ladder. He told me of the time he and his crew had to run rapidly because a huge warehouse suddenly started to collapse, and the sense of intense fear of falling bombs as they worked. I had three uncles on my mother's side of the family who were killed in the trenches, I now have their cards at home, always cheerful and full of hope, but in the late 1960s I could recall my mother's sadness as she recalled her mother receiving the War Office 'death-telegrams' one after the other in the same week as a result of the Battle of the Somme. When at university I met my future wife's grandfather. He had been a regimental sergeant major, and despite his age still behaved like one, and had fought the Turks. He told me of an incident, when prompted by me, of the time a senior officer had ordered him and a few others to shoot anyone who appeared around a derelict building they were watching one night. They shot and killed two, only to discover next morning they were their own men. Like my naval next-door neighbour, he wiped his eyes and told me not a day passed without him feeling 'bad and sad' about that night, and the memory would never go away, and by this time it was nearly half a century later. Finally, I met what I described as an 'old boy' but probably aged less than 50 years who walked with an obvious limp. We were sharing a table with him in the college dining room when someone asked him why he limped. He had, he reluctantly explained, been dropped by parachute into the Arnhem battle, but he was caught swinging from the top of a tree and unable to climb down. He was shot in the foot while swinging there, and he was rescued by a German soldier who climbed the tree under fire. The German struggled to put a tourniquet above his foot, gave him water, helped him down, dragging him along at significant risk to where a German army doctor looked after him. He told us that had this not happened he would have either bled to death or lost his foot. We were speechless, and then he added he hated the Nazi regime but not German people, reminding us that not all Germans were Nazis, and this one had been his Good Samaritan and risked his own life for an enemy soldier.

I finished at university and was undecided as to my future, hearing all these accounts of the recent past which were happening as I was born, I turned against my initial impulses of seeking a career in the military or police, turned to teaching first, then was ordained a priest and later became a professional historian. Oral history can have deep effects on following generations, not only emotionally and psychologically, but recounting personal experience tells us about the realities of history at all conceivable levels. Later in 1969-72 as a curate I spent some time, as mentioned earlier, talking to First World War soldiers in the local British Legion home. Few of them wanted to discuss the trenches, but they were all vociferous about the poverty they suffered before the war, and its continuation when they returned after war had finished. They all agreed that the future in those days looked bleak if not desperate, the rich taking holidays in the Mediterranean coast, while most wondered if they would starve. I recall one old soldier pertinently saying that it had been the same in Germany which had given space for a man like Hitler.

Later, while serving as a parish priest in Woolston, Southampton, I met a man called Bill Fisher who was active in the local church. He had worked in the docks all his life including the war years. I soon heard from mutual friends that Bill had been given the George Cross for his bravery when the docks had been under aerial bombardment. A crane had lifted him as he stood on the hook to be lifted up to the top of a collapsing building and rescued an injured anti-aircraft gunner by bringing him down to ground level by holding him over his shoulder. One day I asked him over a glass of beer how he had lost his finger. He explained that it had been crushed by the chain wires when holding the gunner. He found the hospital that night was too busy, in his words, 'to worry about one crushed finger just hanging by flesh'. He drank some rum, cut it off with a knife and found the pain unbearable. So, he walked into the city and wandered around the common until the pain subsided enough for him to 'feel normal'. He described this to me in the mid-1970s, and left me wondering how he coped, and made me realise how lucky my generation were. Even at the time of the 1962 Cuban Crisis, which is now rapidly becoming history, I can recollect sitting in the local coffee bar with schoolfriends wondering about the future, and hearing that the cliff tunnels we had once penetrated were now guarded by the local garrison, later hearing it had become a safety place for a regional seat for local government. Of life in the trenches, jungles, deserts, at sea or under the sea, high in the sky with bombers and fighter planes much has been written, but hearing from the horse's mouth seems so much more enlightening.

History has become a much-neglected subject which is a mistake because the mistakes of the past are still happening, and history is a good reminder if not prophetic. History for many becomes much more interesting when its features and events are related by those who were there, not so much from the overall perspective of politics, strategies, and policies, but by those on the ground floor or on the frontline. Today, (2025) soon these World War generations will be gone, and a tiny few about 100 years old are still alive, and on VE Day interviewed on television because they are oral history. The time of direct oral history of the war years has virtually gone, but it can still be detected in places in the written word which the following chapters hope to demonstrate.

It is for the reader of the text to evaluate the veracity of any account, and it can be complex. If there is a fight in the playground the teachers may gather the witnesses together to find out what happened and who started the fight and why. It was just one incident, but after hearing the accounts there could be at least five different versions, varying accusations or blame depending on those who are biased on grounds of friendships, some who know, others who were close to the fracas, those who either saw it from a distance, those who were 'in the know', and others based on hearsay and gossip. An experienced teacher should arrive at a satisfactory conclusion, and those who read and enjoy history should be able to detect the genuine oral strands even within a written text. It helps if it is known the writer kept notes or a logbook, but even reminiscent writing by a person who was there comes close to oral history and demands attention.

PUBLISHED ORAL HISTORY AND OR MEMORY HERITAGE

An entire history of the Second World War has been compiled by personal statements found in the archives, and some by interviews, entitled *The World at War, The Landmark of Oral History*.[3] There is no question that it makes for interesting reading, and it follows a chronological sequence of the war years, starting with a brief explanation of the part of history each chapter deals with, then the account unfolds as seen by a vast variety of people, some well-known, others a complete mystery apart from their names. It could be claimed that it is a 'committee book' as its main content is written by many contributors from across the globe and representing all sides of the conflict. Some information comes directly from trusted archives. It is a mixture of genuine recorded oral history and in places what this study refers to as Memory Heritage, and because of the various views expressed makes it not only fascinating but informative.

It is clear that it is often reminiscent history by the nature of the various responses. In this particular book, a U-boat lieutenant on his first command wrote 'I must say in this time we were young…we saw those big merchant ships like animals creeping over the sea and we were eager to sink them, and we didn't think on those poor merchant seamen…but later on when we had been successful we thought about them sometimes, and we had a bad feeling'.[4] This is not a diary note, nor a letter, nor a logbook entry, but a postwar observation. This does not invalidate the content one iota, and it is historically valuable because it offers the viewpoint of the dreaded enemy under the waves. Nevertheless, many say a reliable historian must be cynical, which is to say realistic, and raise the question whether they had 'bad feelings' over their victory or was this personal postwar appeasement. It could have been true that they felt sad, bomber pilots often felt bad about bombing cities, but whether that was true of all U-boat crews, or of a few officers is a question too late to ask. This viewpoint does not detract from the value of the contribution not only because it might reflect the time of war, but it might expose later thinking which is equally important. Memory heritage or personal reminiscence is important in understanding events and human emotions and adds to the importance of history and understanding human nature.

Reminiscent reflections must be treated with caution because they reflect as much as the current day when they were expressed which sometimes, but not always, means the past events under consideration are coloured from the observer's new point of view. The U-boat commander mentioned above feels to the reader that he was perhaps being truthful, though there is a very slight shadow of doubt over their sense of regret, but it still remains useful as it offers insights into the war years, as well as possible reflections afterwards in the postwar era.

This problem emerges in this book more significantly in other accounts, especially those presented by Albert Speer. His postwar literary efforts almost made him popular, appearing as a redeemed one-time Nazi servant, which became his plea at the Nuremberg trial after the Holocaust evidence, writing 'I felt the only out was to tell the judges I felt responsible', in other words it might save him from execution.[5] In this particular book *The World at War, The Landmark of Oral History*, Speer is a major component, quoted some 50 times and his insights are interesting, but it must be borne in mind he had his own agenda. It was well known that Speer used foreign slave labour, many from the concentration camps, and in November 1941 when there was a shortage of military manpower on the Russian front he wrote 'I offered Hitler to use 30,000 of my workmen'.[6] 'My workmen' were slave labourers and he unquestionably knew of the brutality of the prison camps. He attacked the Nazi system for being corrupt when he was part of the system, and he wrote that from listening to Hitler he should have foreseen the danger to the Jews, writing that 'I was running away from my responsibility which was now as a human being'.[7] His observations quoted in the book are often interesting and perceptive, but the reader has to be aware that from the moment Speer, as an intelligent man, saw the war was lost, and everything he wrote was tinged with explanations, excuses, claiming ignorance, all of which constituted a long-term apologia, even appealing to the fact he was only human. He admitted that Stauffenberg's 20 July Plot had sound ethical reasons, then added later that he knew all the plotters, and in their plans, he was down as the proposed armaments minister, and he was only saved from Nazi recriminations because his name was followed by a question mark in the original text.[8]

This book, like many others is valuable as oral reminiscences, but the question of caution must be raised by the reader, especially those notes which were later reflections, and asking if the observations of previous years have different colours for a variety of reasons. Even if this is suspected, as in the case of Speer, it still reflects the person and the postwar era and coming to terms with what had happened.

Another book entitled *Forgotten Voices* uses eye-witness accounts for an authentic insight into various people's accounts during the Blitz and the Battle of Britain, and provides some interesting revelations from the myriads of people involved.[9] In this book the author had searched the Imperial War Museum Sound archives for recordings and information, and the general feeling is that these belong more to oral history than memory heritage. There are some long passages when the contribution is long, and in the case of a German pilot goes back to when he left school in 1931. This particular contributor even goes back to General von Seeckt's days when Germans used Russian land and cooperation to rebuild their military after the Treaty of Versailles.[10] It makes, as does all oral-type history, interesting reading as it is written or spoken by people who were there. In the account by a German pilot, his contribution finishes at the successful German victory over Poland. From the historical point of view, it would have been useful for the reader to know the precise source, whether it was a recorded voice or written statement, and when and where. Nevertheless, the book as a whole gives the impression of real people speaking their minds making it more oral history than later reflections.

Some of the shorter statements also 'sound bells'. One by a civilian in London called John 'Chick' Fowles, who as a boy scout was given the job of looking for the tell-tale signs of unexploded bombs on Hackney Marsh. He only ever found one, but when he looked back, he noted that young people should not have been given such tasks.[11] Another was a member of the Home Guard, a James Lawrence who wrote or said, 'I saw the first bomb that dropped in Ipswich. I saw it leave the plane, and I threw myself down but there was no bang because the bomb had been sabotaged'.[12] This type of oral history helps bring the subject alive because from a Home Guard member to a Boy Scout, it is possible to 'see and feel' the war from the perspective of civilians.

Sometimes these personal insights give a new dimension to history textbooks, because they relate to most readers.

Another published book entitled *The Voice of War* presents the whole global aspect of the Second World War based on original documents and mainly oral history, and those made by some of what may be called 'lesser mortals' (civilians and fighting military) who give the history of this period some pungency and makes it interesting and helps bring history alive.[13] Some major leading figures are quoted, in the first 100 pages Churchill occurs many times, Harold Nicolson, Noël Coward, Galeazzo Ciano. There are famous military names such as Rommel, Adolf Galland, and Gunter Prien [commander of U-boat *47* which sank the *Royal Oak*] and well-known journalists such as William Shirer, Ed Murrow, Ernie Pyle and Alan Moorehead who all had firsthand experience. Then appears a vast number of names from all nationalities, unknown except by their inclusion in this book, giving their accounts and observations. On the one hand the reader can hear Churchill's views, on the other the personal feelings of a civilian who was close to one of the first V-1 rockets which fell near his home in London. It covers well-known battles on land, at sea, and in the air, ranging across the globe.

This book offers insights into the value of this form of oral history, and this exploration will offer four unusual examples from that text. The first curious one was by the Australian born journalist and writer Alan Moorehead, who wrote about the frequent social conflict between Australian and British soldiers with their different backgrounds and histories. It was, he argued, a matter of time, even though the Australians were fond of Britain, and he detected the British liked Australia, but sometimes they did not work together happily. He noted that 'it was usually the officers of both armies who rubbed one another up the wrong way. The men got together as soon as they began to understand one another'.[14] This reflection by Moorehead draws out a very human condition that those who work and fight together soon become like a family, an essential ingredient, not just in war but in life generally.

The second choice came as a stunning surprise, as it related to an account by an SS officer called Kurt Gerstein.[15] He described in his report a visit to concentration camps to see how Zyklon B gas was used. It is simply horrifying to read and acts as a reminder of how evil a regime can become. The shock is to discover that Kurt Gerstein had joined the SS as a Christian spy, who told the Swedes he was investigating what was happening, but they tended to ignore his information. He was condemned to death as a war criminal but hanged himself first. Two days late the Swedes wrote confirming his innocence. Even as a professional historian this writer sat stunned when he read this oral piece of information.

The third selection is from a Norwegian parachutist called Oluf Olsen who volunteered to be dropped back into Norway to help the underground resistance.[16] The whole account describes him choosing to jump in dangerously high winds, his chute was caught by the plane's tail dragging him along and eventually falling to the ground with a twisted and damaged parachute. He was damaged with bruises and a dislocated knee, all of which he fixed to his best ability and hobbled down to the road where he hitched a lift from a car carrying German soldiers. He wrote his knee felt better when their car drew away from his stop. This is one man's account of a nightmare in which he showed considerable bravery and courage, and the nerve to hitch a lift from the enemy.

The final choice represents a normal person's fear and disgust. It is related by a German called Claus Fuhrmann, a civilian in Berlin as Russian soldiers took over the city.[17] He was a civilian and with his wife was trying to survive and stay alive, and he was conscious as he made his way home to Bunny his wife that women were being raped on street corners by Russian soldiers. She did not escape their attention, and two soldiers made it clear what was about to happen. Bunny told her husband not to watch, when it was over, one of the soldiers 'patted me [Claus] on the shoulder: '*Nix Angst! Russki Solday gut!*' This was a sharp reminder not just of the barbarity of war but how far human behaviour can be degraded, the produce of war.

A research oral historian Max Arthur, author of some 25 history books before he died, wrote several based on oral history. Published in 2002 was *Forgotten Voices of The Great War*.[18] This book dug into the archives for recorded messages and interviews of people who fought in the Great War, now well over a hundred years ago. They were mainly men and boys who fought in a war of attrition with the countless loss of lives which from any perspective was a heedless waste of a generation, such were the numbers on both sides of the divide. These oral contributions underline the sheer rawness of this major industrialised series of battles, and where it was all too clear that death was their constant companion. These are oral observations by those who fought in this bitter war and a sharp reminder to politicians who turn to war to resolve their perceived errors or policies.

This study will select three incidents from this book which caught this writer's eye. The first was from a chaplain assisting a medical officer when a British soldier and German helping one another came into the medical tent together. 'Our man said to the doctor, "Here's a job I made for you doctor, and he made this one for me". What could you do with men like that! They were grand'.[19] It was a feature of this war that soldiers had to fight to the death, but the hatred was not so deep as it was when fighting the Nazi regime. The second choice was when the men were told to stand up and line the road because the King was coming by in a car. Private Raynor Taylor said the officers cheered, but not the men who remained silent, noting that 'after a period in the front line, you weren't in any mood to cheer anybody'.[20] Perhaps some may have thought, knowing the Kaiser and the British Royal family were related, that they were all too responsible for the mess everyone was in. It was the same thought which crossed Henry V's mind prior to Agincourt, according to Shakespeare. Finally, Private William Holmes recalled two newly arrived recruits aged between 16 and 17 years of age were distraught when they realised that they had turned up just as an attack was about to happen. Being scared they disappeared and were designated as deserters, and they were to be shot at dawn from men drawn from Private Holmes' Platoon as they were their new members. Four men were told to shoot the boys the next day with one bullet to the head the other to the heart. The families were not told the facts, just that they died in action. This almost defies belief; war is brutal but the lack of compassion of senior officers for terrified youngsters was even worse. Many books have been written on the causes of the First World War, the course of the war, the strategies deployed, developing new weapons such as tanks and planes, but the majority of fighting was hand to hand in the war of attrition of the trenches. The truth of which touched nearly every family in all the engaged countries as can be seen by the memorials from cities to the smallest villages, and the reality for the front-line soldiers is best conveyed by this type of oral history and serves as history's stark reminder that war is best avoided. On this subject of oral history Max Arthur wrote many books. In 2005 he wrote *Last Post* which was another study of the First World War, this time he interviewed veterans who survived, the youngest being 104, the oldest 109.[21] It is a first-class book, but because of the time gap tends to be more about the memory heritage and reminiscences, which is a step down from Oral history, but close enough (as these men were there) to be read with care and interest. Such were the memories they must have felt it was only yesterday and should be taken seriously but with a historical degree of caution.

Max Arthur used research efforts to explore those who fought at sea and those in the air. His book on the Royal Navy spans in detail the views of sailors from 1914 to 1945, including the interbellum years.[22] The book is over 500 pages long, packed with personal accounts which portray a picture of Royal Naval life during these difficult years. Such was the desperation for manpower in 1914 a man recorded how he tried to join the navy giving his age as sixteen years five months, but he was in fact much younger, and the 'recruiting officer advised me to go outside and have another birthday'.[23] Many teenagers were influenced to change their ages because as another observer noted 'the poster of Lord Kitchener was everywhere pointing his finger at you'.[24]

In another incident one sailor describes what it was like to be under enemy shellfire, describing how the captain on the bridge was killed, and another shell penetrating to a room where 56 marines were preparing to go ashore. 'Forty-nine were killed. There was just one big heap of arms and legs. My friend had his head blown off. He'd only just got married on the weekend before we left'.[25] In this and many other contributions the reality of the war years is accurately portrayed. Nor was it peaceful after the Great War as many of them travelled overseas and into trouble or witnessed brutality. One seaman, a gunner called Stan Smith had sailed to the Bosphorus 'to clear up' Gallipoli then on to Baku where he was captured by the Bolsheviks. As a prisoner he was forced with others to watch the execution of dissidents, men women and children. He recalled that 'one by one they slit the women up the middle to about the chest bone, disembowelled them and left them standing until they'd done the whole crowd of women'… 'then they made some of the men put their arms into buckets of acid'.[26] This must have been an appalling experience, not least because the Royal Navy was not technically at war.

During the Second World War Max Arthur found recordings and interviews skilfully put together as if one is reading a Royal Navy history, but as seen by men of all ranks who were there. There are observations in the retreat from Dunkirk, the sinking of the *Hood* followed by the *Bismarck*, to convoy patrol and the U-boat warfare. For many this form of oral history brings history to life, and makes the subject not only more readable, but makes the reader learn the lesson that history must be read in order not to repeat past errors and blunders.

This was not his first book as in 1993 he had produced a similar book on the RAF starting in its earliest days as the RFC.[27] The observations of the participants cover the Battle of Britain, to the offensive, bomber and coastal command. It is global as it covers many parts of the world and stretches beyond 1945 and right up to what some historians might call current times such as the Middle East problems, the Falklands, and the Gulf War. He also covers many aspects of personnel, including the memory of Aircraftwoman Olive Snow recalling one occasion when in her work as a parachute packer one of the women failed to do the rigging in the right way and the parachute failed resulting in a death. The woman involved was moved, but she wrote 'that death cast a gloom over the place for a while, and it really made us think more about the work'.[28] They were well away from the 'frontline', but the demands were high as the slightest error could bring disaster for someone else.

Flight Lieutenant Lucian Ercolani described the horror of trying to return to base with his bomber on fire; ditching into the sea, he found himself submerged, pinned down by the instrument panel and unable to escape. 'I definitely thought I'd had it then and there and that I was finished'.[29] He was fortunate that the plane popped to the surface, and he escaped, but in a few words, he described what must be for everyone a sheer nightmare. In another observation Flight Lieutenant Bill Reid was wounded, the plane was losing height, but he kept quiet about his wound to stop the crew being terrified and later landed in Norfolk where he was rushed to hospital.[30] This wounded pilot was first thinking of his crew before himself, and in some circumstances, war can bring out the best in some individuals. Many airmen became PoWs, one moment having tea in their mess, then a few hours later on the ground in enemy territory. There are many references in the book to their prison life and escape attempts. Many films have been made on this aspect of the war, but none as good as hearing it directly from 'the horse's mouth' or, to use another expression, 'the Gospel truth'.

There are many such books which can be found on library and shop shelves, and they can make history that much more interesting and meaningful for the general reader and the professional historian alike. There are too many to mention, let alone comment on, but one which caught the eye was *Voices from the Luftwaffe* which used similar techniques to convey the views and feelings of those on the other side of the divide.[31] It expressed the views and observations of many witnesses recording their feelings as events unfolded. Curiously he mentioned a German pilot Ulrich Steinhilper who is mentioned later in this study (p.137) as his autobiography was deemed worthy of reading as his reflections appear sound and true to the day.[32]

Many publications are there to be read, some are more useful than others, depending on what the reader is seeking. One major effort was made by the writer Travis Elborough covering the whole of the twentieth century.[33] It is a compilation of many small 'bits and pieces' from well-known people to the unknown, from a selection of letters, diaries and journals. It is not the sort of book enjoyable enough to read from cover to cover, but useful for research. If anyone is curious about the impact of the Great War, the rise of Oswald Mosley, the Second World War, and to the end of the century, there are some 'titbits' of information which can be quite revealing. They offer what many of the public were thinking at the time, including some well-known names from the wider world as well as the more intellectual thinkers, a book of reactions.

Oral History and the heritage of memory, allows the reader to explore the past from many different angles, not only from both sides of the divide, but the bombed people on the ground and the pilots above. A careful selection of such publications offers the viewpoints and feelings of the top command to the fighting soldier and sailor, and the public watching with hope and fear; in short it brings history alive.

Chapter Two

Letters Offer Insights

INTRODUCTION

Personal letters written by people at the time events were unfolding are always of interest for students of Oral History. The best ways for gaining insights of past days are often personal ones to family and friends who were not anticipating being read outside the relationship and certainly not for publishing. Official letters, often found in archives, usually state known facts, and rarely disclose the inner-thinking and personal thoughts of the writer. Personal letters are by their very nature private and more like whispered asides in a family gathering.

Two of the selected sources come from virtually unknown sources, one a German soldier on the Eastern Front, and the other from a German officer who worked for Rommel in 1941. Two more German sources are also noted, Rommel's personal letters to his family, and Himmler's letters to his wife and daughter. The American General George Patton's family letters are explored and the well-known British intellectual George Orwell with his interesting observations.

What makes them so useful in understanding the past is not so much the revealing of historical facts, but personal letters take us into the 'mindset' of the individual about their feelings, their priorities, and the atmosphere of the times through which they lived. The study starts with the feared and hated figure of Heinrich Himmler who comes across as a loving and caring if not tender person, and for this writer they were simply astonishing. The selected figures from three nationalities offer insights into the minds of their writers at a personal level, and they are a stark reminder that these written artefacts from the past open new doors of understanding past events, as if we were there with them.

HEINRICH AND MARGA HIMMLER
THE BANALITY OF EVIL

The Background

This section is about discovered personal letters between Heinrich Himmler and his wife and his daughter.[1] They may be of interest to those studying Himmler, but they raise the deeper question of how a man perceived through these letters could in reality be the epitome of pure evil. Some people who met Himmler before the war made all kinds of judgement on this figure of growing power in Nazi Germany. Many saw him as impeccably polite, mild mannered and of a pleasant nature. The historian John Toland wrote that 'cleanliness was a fetish with him, and he gargled and washed himself throughout the day. He was a man of exact habits, parsimonious, neat and careful, and blessed with no originality, common sense or intuition…in the acid words of SS General Paul Hausser, who had helped him organise the Waffen-SS, the one-time chicken farmer was a 'fantastic idealist with both feet planted several inches above the earth, a right queer bird'.[2]

In late 1927 Himmler met the woman who felt right for him, an older but blonde and blue-eyed Aryan, called Margarete, who used the shorter version of Marga. She was a nurse working in a private clinic at first earning more than Himmler, and they had two children. Marga continued to work as a nurse during the war years. It was not plain sailing as Himmler's secretary Hedwig Potthast soon became of personal interest, but they did not become intimate until about 1940, probably when he was satisfied that she was a 'true Aryan'.* They also had children and it appears Marga was aware, unhappy, but accepted the situation. Both remained loyal to him to the end.

---

* Himmler nevertheless carried out extensive research into her ancestry even into the early years of the war. See Manvell, Roger and Fraenkel, Heinrich, *Heinrich Himmler: The Sinister Life of the Head of the SS and Gestapo* (London: Skyhorse Publishing, 2007), p.59.

He was, next to Hitler, probably the most feared and venomous person within Germany and its occupied territories, but from the family letters, apart from the occasional mutual anti-Semitic remarks, and Marga's comments on his continued absence on Party demands, there is only the feeling of a married couple in love. The letters are seemingly full of mutual adoration, often tinged with family humour. It will never be known how much Marga really or precisely knew about the nature of her husband's work.

He is now known as a dangerous racist, and a man with his obsessive views on behaviour and lifestyle who physically imposed his views across many nations. Through the concentration camp system and mass murders he authorised, Himmler ensured he was responsible for a total and vicious suppression of those selected candidates on his list. He claimed that criminals suffered from biological defects, he attacked abortionists, homosexuals, Romas and all gypsies, clergy, Freemasons, Jehovah's Witnesses, Jews, and anyone who did not fit his endless list. He saw these groups as a national threat, explaining that 'We are a country in the heart of Europe surrounded by open borders, surrounded by a world that is becoming more and more Bolshevized, and increasingly taken over by the Jew.'[3] Few were safe from his judgment.

It was under his leadership there were experiments with Zyklon B in Auschwitz and developing industrialised mass murder, enabling Rosenberg to tell a press conference of 'an impending biological elimination of the whole of European Jewry'.[4] He was able to issue his directives from the safety of his desk, but he still found time to visit concentration camps, at Treblinka and Sobibor where a mass execution of young Jewish girls was made for his personal observation. He watched medical experiments making suggestions for progress, and he was always interested in the work results in terms of money and productivity. In January 1943 Himmler visited Warsaw, where he ordered the destruction of the ghetto.

He was ultimately responsible for the deaths of millions of innocent men, women, children, and babies. He knew it was wrong, and many histories of this era refer to his efforts to destroy the gas-chambers, and he tried to communicate with the enemy. Interestingly the historian Longerich pointed out that a recent archival discovery indicated that Churchill had received some missive from Himmler which he promptly destroyed.[5] He held clandestine dealings with the well-known Swede Bernadotte in the hope of 'extracting something out of the disaster for himself even at the end', playing 'a double game'.[6] On the day he went to the bunker for Hitler's last birthday he was still making contact with Bernadotte and a representative of the World Jewish Congress, Norbet Masur. Dönitz as Hitler's appointed successor, quickly disassociated himself from Himmler, who tried to escape in disguise, but he was captured by the British and bit on his concealed cyanide capsule.

The Letters
The modern reader of these letters may well be bemused at the way they address one another. During their initial courtship they start *Dear Herr Himmler*, signed *Very Cordially yours, Frau M. Siegroth*, (16 October 1927). Within a year it becomes *My dear, good Marga*, concluding *Yours Heini*. As they become more intimate, they deploy a series of nicknames in what may be called a 'leg-pulling' game, with Marga addressing him as *Dickkopp* which is close to *Dickkopf* (Dickhead) which can mean 'headstrong'.

The publication of these letters is lengthy as for a few years they wrote every day and most of the letters are somewhat vacuous, but the early ones are full of love, adoration and full of compliments to one another. They discuss marriage plans. Marga admits she find's Himmler's family difficult, and they both deride Jewish people. As early as 6 May 1928 Marga is writing that *Darling, I cannot comprehend why you let the party rule your life*. It is because of these letters that research discovered that Marga had been married before, not that it is or was of any importance.

They were married on 3 July 1928 with Himmler's job in life described as 'Licensed Agronomist', with him writing to Marga, *You dearest beloved little wife, Today I received your sweet letter. How I would like to hold you and kiss you for this letter.* When Gudrun was born a series of nicknames appeared from *little scamp* to *puppy*. On 14 October Himmler wrote to Marga about some mutual friends, writing *I cannot keep living with them. He is afraid for the Jews, nonetheless, they are endlessly kind and good.* For Himmler and obviously other Nazi anti-Semites, the Jews were not only subhuman, but in serious doubt were those people who had any sympathy for the growing plight of Jews.

Himmler and Marga had adopted a fair-haired blue-eyed son (his SS father had been killed in a street fight) called Gerhard von der Ahé (1928-2010) and his family nickname mentioned in the letters became Bubi.* These letters if read without knowing the parents would sound as if they reflected kind loving people full of affection and care helped by a family sense of humour.

When Himmler started his affair there is no sign of the affectionate letters changing, though there are huge gaps, whether because they were lost or not written. In the publication of these letters are portions of her journal. This gap occurred during 1938 when Himler was becoming more important and also involved with his mistress. There are occasional hints in Marga's journal and on 3 July 1938 she wrote *I have been married ten years today. H. is away on a trip, but he telephoned. Despite the happiness of marriage, I have had to do without a lot when it comes to marriage.* Nevertheless, she had been thrilled when in the May of that year she was visited by the Führer.[7]

During the war she wrote (11 June 1940), *My Dear good husband, I hope you do not have to see too many horrible things.* The modern reader would be astonished as hearing Himmler addressed as 'good', and later he mentioned when he was away various places in occupied areas in which he explained to Marga that he was busy organising the

---

* Gerhard later saw two days' active service, was sentenced to 25 years hard labour by the Russians but returned in 1955.

administration. Checking the dates and places where he happened to be, reveals several times that he was busy orchestrating the massacre of thousands of Jews and others, often watching the process.

He was also busy with his second wife and forgot to send greetings on Marga's wedding anniversary. Nevertheless, it is difficult to detect these tensions in the letters where love and affection continue unabated. Even when his mistress was giving birth to their first child, Himmler wrote a loving letter and sent some sweets. Marga knew what was going on, but there is next to no anger expressed in the letters, which could not have been because they expected them to be published, it was a form of acceptance. Even in the last letters the love and affection remained. In the final letter he wrote to Marga and Gudrun, before he escaped only to bite on a cyanide tablet, he signed off with *Heil Hitler! With love Your Pappi* (17 April 1945). It was the only time he wrote *Heil Hitler* in this personal correspondence, as if emphasising where his central loyalty dwelt.

As noted earlier these private letters between a notorious mass murderer and his wife are not hugely important unless researching the man Himmler. On the other hand, it offers a stark warning about us human beings. The danger of passing judgement on a brief meeting like Stephen Roberts, an Australian professor who met Himmler and the other Nazis in the interbellum years. Roberts later wrote 'Personally I found him [Himmler] much kindlier and much more thoughtful for his guests…a man of exquisite courtesy and still interested in the simple things of life. He has none of the pose of those Nazis who act as demigods'.[8] Murderers do not necessarily look like murderers or even behave as if they could. The warning is that Himmler was driven by an evil racial ideology which he helped develop and which cost the lives of millions and suffering beyond that, even if he was *my dear good husband Heini*. It is a strange piece of revealing Oral History.

A GERMAN SOLDIER'S LETTERS FROM RUSSIA

Introduction

Many families have letters from relatives who played various roles during the twentieth century. This writer has cards sent from the First World War trenches by uncles who never returned home. One German family came across a vast collection of some 500 letters written by their grandfather who served on the notorious Eastern front as an ordinary soldier during the Second World War. They were found in 'grandfather's old post-letters kept by his wife'. They were read and carefully put in order. They are deeply personal but nevertheless provide an insight into an ordinary soldier's life and suffering during these years. They were evidently not deemed interesting enough to find a commercial or even academic publisher, but they can be found in Amazon's publications.[9] However, they are important because they reflect Oral History as he wrote down his thoughts on a regular basis, offering serious perceptions from a soldier who missed his family. They do not reveal any new information, and he would have been careful how he expressed himself, as he and his comrades would have been aware of the censorship office. As the grandson was told, 'my grandfather wrote as he spoke'.[10] They reflect his views, his sense of optimism and hopes for the future, his tasks in the war, and what many such letters seldom enter into any depth, his feelings of separation from those he loved.

His name was Joseph (Josef) Chervatin, he born in Labin in 1903, in 1927 he married Alma and moved to Ahlen, Westphalia. He was a musician and accountant by which he earned his living. In 1934 their only child Hans was born, to whom he refers to as Hansi in his letters. In October 1941 Josef volunteered for service in Wehrmacht joining the 329th Infantry Division formed in December 1941, part of Army Group North, he was then aged about 38 years of age. *Whenever he is quoted directly in this summary the date of the letter is in brackets.*

Love of Family

There is hardly a single letter which does not express the pain he feels by being separated from his wife and son. One of his consistent communications is about his seeking leave to go home for a few days or weeks to be with his family. Time and time again he wrote about his requests for leave and his expectancy that it should soon be his turn. It was a frustrating issue, obviously not helped by the pressures of war, and on one occasion he asked his wife to make a request for him to have leave; this issue was constantly in his correspondence (See 31.3.1942 and 4.7.1942).

On one occasion he raised a major concern in February 1944 that his son Hans (Hansi) should go to an academic school not the suggested 'Adolf Hitler School'. He was forthright on this issue and felt it important, but carefully expressed the view an academic school was better for his future, undoubtedly aware this had to pass a possible censor.

He was more worried about the bombing raids by the English, and in typical German style referred to them as English and not British. When he referred to the English bombing raids against 'our cities', he noted that 'the English will probably experience our wrath soon' (27.4. 1942). He was deeply annoyed with 'the Tommies, (13.3.1943) wondering why British bombers could so easily penetrate German airspace, and he no sympathy for these 'English bastards when they come down' (6.12.1943), a feeling shared by the British over German airmen.

All these letters clearly indicate a man who was loving to his family and regretted being away, especially when they too were in danger. His sense of concern and longing to be back home are a major feature of his personality. This will be returned to in the section which explores his apparent optimism, which was reflected in giving his family a sense of hope and confidence, but first it is important to explore his war experience.

War Experience

It is clear that possibly because of his age and civilian experience he was rarely if ever on the front line, which in Second World War history is known to have been one of the bitterest areas of combat and marked by appalling atrocities by both sides. He had a variety of office-type posts and some military involvement.

As with all those on the Eastern Front the Russian winter came as a shock, when the Germans stood close to Moscow the winter was one of the worse ever, with some histories pointing out that the only worse winter in known history was when Napoleon tried to occupy Russia. Josef wrote 'what luck we finally survived the winter. Hopefully we won't have to go through a second one' (9.4.1942); his predictions or hopes were wrong and a few months later (6.11.1942) he wrote 'bad frost here, about 6 to 8 degrees below Celsius … ten days later frost gone leaving deep mud, the frost was much more pleasant'. He mentioned when the snow was so deep and frozen, they could walk on it, then it would suddenly thaw, and they were faced with deep mud and water. Despite this he told his wife their quarters were always comfortable, and they were well fed, but tending to miss his cigarettes. Whether he was telling the truth or trying to stop his wife worrying is another question. When he first arrived his first duty was standing guard every third to fourth night for two hours in the cold (9.3.1942). From his letters the reader learns that thy were attacked by Russian aircraft, and a comrade had a bullet in his stomach and died (21.5.42).

Not all his quarters he admitted were safe, and he wrote (9.6.1942) 'We have got a new kind of enemy here in the Russian forests. Lately there have been a lot of poisonous snakes, two kinds of vipers. It can't get any worse here. It's hard to imagine what you have to fight against here. Apart from Bolsheviks and partisans, it was ice, snow, cold, and mud, then lice, mosquitoes, and other vermin, and now the nasty snakes. But despite everything, we keep our courage and our heads high'.

They were bombed, and a friend called Hugo Hapke was wounded, 'so we sleep in our uniforms and have not seen a bed for months'

(12.6.1942). By the August of 1942 he was suffering from diarrhoea (15.8.1942) and desperate for some cigarettes. He held a variety of tasks from traffic control, where they had to make everyone identify themselves, to working in accountancy. He was sent on a training session (14.1.1943), which included night drills, and seeing new weapons appearing. In early 1943 (1.3.1943) he was made a lance corporal and later in the same year (17.12.1943) was corporal (Gefreiter).

He was for a time attached to a draft board (24.8.1943) seeking recruits, but much of the time he was involved in accountancy work. He would make occasional comments to his wife. He was sorry to hear of Mussolini's downfall (12.9.1943), and in new quarters he wrote (25.11.1943) explaining they were now housed in a Jewish house, 'many millionaires amongst them', but he had heard bad news from the unit, many of whom were dead. In December 1943 (26.12.1943) he visited hospital to see a wounded comrade, and he was horrified at the number there, and how battered they were. He added at the beginning of the new year (3.2.1944) that the news from his unit was not good, telling his wife that 'I'm lucky I'm here at the detachment'.

His Optimism

One of the features of his letters is his continuous optimism which is difficult to explain. Either he generally believed the Germans could win the war, or he trusted Hitler and Goebbels' speeches too much, or he was trying to comfort his wife. This optimism was more understandable in the early years, but less so after such events as the Battle of Stalingrad. There is also the distinct possibility that in his detachment he could not be that informed of the realities of what was happening elsewhere.

He wrote not long after he arrived that 'I think it will soon be over for the Russians' (26.3.1942), which many thought was a possibility and understandable. The German advance into Russia, helped by Stalin's refusal to believe Hitler would invade looked likely to succeed. He later added that 'we won't have to go through a second winter, Adolf Hitler will see to that' (9.4.1942). Perhaps, at this time, he was like so many others seeming to think Hitler was something of a military genius. He thought 'we can use the good weather to finally beat the Russians (20.4.42), and later 'In our opinion the main fighting force of the Russians is already broken'.

His confidence was boosted outside of the Russian war, when he heard (15.8.1942) about convoys destroyed in the Mediterranean, writing 'the English and Americans will soon have no ships left,' undoubtedly prompted by Goebbels' propaganda speeches, and like so many others underestimating the industrial power of America, which Goebbels and others thought was mainly their ability to build kitchenware. When he heard of the disastrous poorly prepared Dieppe Raid, he wrote 'it will probably happen to them every time, should they try something else' (20.8.1942).

However, for the more astute, the years 1942 to 1943 indicated the war was not so much in Germany's favour, and the sheer manpower of the Soviet Union, assisted by American supplies brought in by the Royal Navy was shifting the balance away from Nazi-Germany success. In late 1942 (25.10.1942) he 'heard a rumour [and it was only rumour] that Ribbentrop and Molotov are negotiating armistice hoping it happens in near future'. For the ordinary German soldier, especially in some areas such as the Eastern Front, it must have felt depressing, and by 1942 (20.1.1943) he wrote 'this year the war in the east will be decided. Either we win this year, or we go kaputt, but that will probably be out of the question', like most still hoping for the best. But two months later he wrote to his wife (7.3.1943) admitting that his prediction the war would end soon was wrong. Six months later (1.8.1943) on a return journey from leave he described to his wife that 'many comrades were very depressed and no longer believed in victory. I claimed the opposite and said the decisive battle would start in the West this year'. Even as disaster was approaching those on the Eastern Front, the growing bombing raids on German cities, and the threat of a second front in Western Europe grew he still seemed to have hope. For the reader of these letters, it is easy to feel that he was not only hoping for the best but possibly trying to give hope to his wife who was also in danger from the bombing raids.

In the opening months of 1944 (3.2.1944.) he wrote that he was hoping that when winter was over it would be quieter in the east, adding 'we believe something will be done against England' before they and the Americans land in the West. No doubt boosted by Goebbels' propaganda and out of sheer hope he wrote in mid-1944 (28.7.1944) as the Allies were breaking out of Normandy, that 'at last, we will achieve victory and, with it, peace, which will then richly compensate us for everything we had to bear. All will be well one day' and a month later (2.8.44) 'we've got the Russians on the run again', which may have related to a local fight but did not reflect the overall scenario.

A month later (17.9.1944) he wrote that 'in the general war situation, things do not look very favourable for us on all fronts right now,' but even his flagging hopes were boosted (15.11.44) when he referred to Goebbels' speech and the wonder weapons (V1, V2s,) writing that we must win the last round, 'otherwise it will be the downfall for us all'.

By the start of 1945 (21.1.1945) he wrote that 'we have just heard the latest Wehrmacht report. Things are not looking good on our eastern border, but still things have suddenly improved for us in the West', which was probably a reference to the well-known Battle of the Bulge when there had been a German counterattack in the Ardennes which failed. When this battle turned against the Germans his hopeful messages stopped with a letter to his wife (6.2.45) stating that 'You can expect a little more humanity from the Americans and English than from the Russians'.

It was not long after this letter that Josef was taken prisoner by the Russians and became part of their notorious hard labour system. At the end of this book of personal letters, Josef described how he and two others escaped from their latest labour-site in Eastern Europe, crossed into Russian occupied Eastern Germany and then into West Germany, and was reunited with his family on 3 September 1949, after an absence of five and a half years.

Final Note

These frank and honest letters written by an ordinary German soldier on a regular basis (during the war years) to his beloved family expose the hopes and fears of a soldier on the dreaded Eastern Front, exposing not just his situation, but his main concern being the welfare of his family, at times offering hope when there was little to offer. Many soldiers on all sides of the conflict would have felt the pain of family division more than is often realised. Despite the possible censorship of personal mail, these letters were frank and honest, and because the original letters have survived, this form of Oral History has taken us into the mind of the ordinary soldier with his hopes and fears. They are not critical history documents, but they are essential reading for understanding the hopes and fears of the ordinary soldier in conflict.

ROMMEL'S PERSONAL LETTERS

THE DESERT FOX

Background

Johannes Erwin Eugen Rommel is probably one of the best-known senior generals of the Second World War, often known as the Desert Fox. He was even admired by many of his British opponents and respected for his dynamic skills, and the rumours that he was humane with captured prisoners. Many books have been written on him. He was a supporter of Hitler until near the end of the war, and whether he changed his views because the war was being lost or whether he took time to recognise the evils of the regime remains unknown. It is equally vague as to how he knew about the 20 July Plot and whether he had just heard a rumour. By this stage he was a national if not an international hero, so he was quietly eliminated to avoid Nazi embarrassment with an execution.

His military career in the Second World War started with him guarding Hitler's field headquarters during the Polish invasion, but in the Battle of France he led a panzer division with considerable success by using his tactics of surprise developed from his experience in the First World War. In February 1941 he became commander of the *Afrika Korps* from where his status as a leading general blossomed. At first it was successful, the First Battle of El Alamein, the Battle of Alam el Halfa and the threat of breaking into Egypt. There followed defeat at the Second Battle of El Alamein, the retreat west through North Africa, but he had an embarrassing victory against the then untested American troops at Kasserine Pass. Probably the climate and stress had made him physically unwell, and he returned to Germany handing over the command to General von Arnim. On 23 July 1943 he was moved to Greece as commander of Army Group E but was promptly, within two days, called back to Berlin on the fall of Mussolini. This meant Italy had become a problem and who should be in charge, Rommel or Kesselring. Rommel wanted a defensive line north of Rome and Kesselring wanted to fight for every metre from the south which naturally had a greater appeal to Hitler.

In November 1943 he was deployed to the English Channel coast to prepare defences against an Allied sea-invasion, undoubtedly Hitler was aware of Rommel's reputation internationally and wanted him associated with the defences. After the invasion an allied plane attacked his staff car near Sainte-Foy-de-Montgommery (of all names), and he was seriously injured, hospitalised then soon the Nazi-arranged death.

Rommel's Oral History

Rommel spent many hours writing his own military diary, at times writing it out more fully as if preparing for a book. He had already written a treatise on *Infantry Tactics* from his experience in the First World War and may well have had his eye on another publication. This appeared over 70 years ago in 1953 under the title *The Rommel Papers*, which was edited and introduced by the famous historian B.H.

Liddell-Hart with assistance from Rommel's wife Lucie-Maria and his son Manfred with further assistance from General Fritz Bayerlein.[11] His son Manfred explained in the book that following Rommel's death that they had a considerable quantity of documents ranging from high command to situation reports to family letters. He also knew that in the latter stage of his life Rommel wanted it all to be as objective as possible, and on his return from Africa had spent hours working on these documents. It took Manfred and his mother considerable effort to keep these papers safe from potential pillaging.

There are two aspects about this book which make for interesting reading for those interested in Oral History seeking the veracity of those days. For those whose nations once opposed Nazi Germany it is curious to read the almost day-by-day encounters as seen by a well-known active German commander who saw action in Western Europe, North Africa where his name is almost legendry, then he was in Italy, and then back to France. He encompassed many areas of land fighting during this war and the modern-day reader can see it through his eyes. He comes through as a man of clever tactics and even strategy, a realist tinged with optimism, and just a touch of the 'adventurer'. This first aspect is of great importance to students of tactics and strategy and warfare.

The second feature belongs more to the letters he wrote and received because they are cleverly interspersed based on datelines, sometimes written at moments of success, or under stress, and even at moments of admitting defeat or a possible disaster. His letters to his wife tell us more about the character of the man Rommel and his inner thinking, as well as providing a précis of the ups and downs of the war.

As the battle of France was underway, he wrote this to his wife whom he called Lu, that 'everything is wonderful. I am ahead of my neighbours…had bare three hours sleep and an occasional meal'.[12] For Rommel like many commanders he seemed to enjoy the conflict, and his ambition shone through when he was pleased to say he was ahead of other German troops. A fortnight later he was still mentioning lack of sleep but pleased to say his 'division has had a blazing success' as they advanced into France 40 miles in one night and told Lu not to worry about him personally.[13] He became internationally famous in North Africa, but it was in France with his rapid thrusts that he drew attention to his leadership qualities. He even predicted to his wife the war in France would soon be over, and his estimate was close to the mark. By 7 June he told Lu that there were 'More signs of disintegration on the other side…and I slept like top'.[14] There is no doubt that she could have read all this in the newspaper reports, which in her replies she occasionally mentions, but Rommel as a husband who obviously cared for his wife and family was providing a précis of events 'from him-to-her'. Like most commanders and all people, he revelled in success, writing that 'two glorious days in pursuit, first south, then south-west. A roaring success. 45 miles yesterday'.[15]

In the meantime, the book covers his war diary on a daily basis consuming some 90 pages, whereas his short missives to Lu would barely take a few pages, but they indicate the German sweeping and speedy success which even surprised the German High Command and Hitler, who was thereby judged to be a military genius, but because of men like Rommel.

He only had a short home-leave because he was sent to North Africa to fight with the Italians against the British forces. For a time, many of his letters to his wife reflected the same pattern of success, the diary notes giving the precise details, but his letters indicating that he was a driven man, always optimistic and very sure of himself and his men in the *Afrika Korps*, all 'enjoying the sunshine'.[16] By April 1941 it felt to Rommel the North African venture would be as successful as France, admitting he had taken a risk by ignoring orders from 'Tripoli and Rome, and perhaps Berlin too…we've already reached our first objective' telling his wife 'you will understand that I can't sleep for happiness' and that he had received congratulations from the Führer.[17]

Occasionally in the early days around Tobruk, he was beginning to recognise it would not be like driving through France, telling Lu that 'the British are very stubborn and had a great deal of artillery'.[18] As things became tougher, he was critical about his Italian allies, stating that 'there's little reliance to be placed on the Italian troops. They're extremely sensitive to enemy tanks and – as in 1917 – quick to throw up [*throw in* is better] the sponge'.[19] It soon became known that Rommel and many other German officers were contemptuous of the Italian fighting, for reasons not part of this study. When the tide of war started to turn against him, he referred to the 'failure of a major Italian formation'.[20] Later he admitted 'the Italian troops give us a lot of worry'.[21] His relationship with the Italians was never happy, and he mentions this many times in his letters to his wife. Later he would write the 'trouble is with Rome, who don't agree with the way I am running things and who would be pleased to see us get out of Cyrenaica'.[22]

It was not as plain sailing as he wanted, and he complained to Lu that he had 'received a rocket from Brauchitsch, the reason why completely passes my comprehension'.[23] He was a man who wanted matters dealt with by the man on the spot. In Britain the Chief of the General Staff, Alan Brooke, was forever unknowingly agreeing with Rommel when Churchill kept complaining about the lack of progress by his commanders, Alan Brooke insisting they had to trust the commander in the field. Rommel would clash with others, not least Halder and later in Italy with Kesselring. It is clear that Rommel had a good sense of humour, when complaining to Lu he had a bad stomach he described a fowl he had eaten 'which must have come from Rameses II's chicken run'.[24]

As the going became tougher against the British his optimism became more cautious telling Lu 'I hope we get through it'.[25] The battle was becoming harder, and on their wedding anniversary he found time to tell Lu 'I want to thank you for all the love and kindness through the years', indicating he had a genuine loving relationship, writing this as he faced a difficult battle. He was still scoring successes but telling Lu 'The British will not give up if I know them'.[26]

By his second year in Africa he recognised that the going was tougher, but his letters continued to show a high degree of optimism, which was fair enough as his forces were still proving successful in the various clashes, and in June 1942, he told his wife that 'the enemy is breaking up', and he was hoping to break through into Egypt, which was beginning to look possible.[27] He noticed at this time, as he slept in his car, that the Allied air force was beginning to hold the upper hand, and made the observation they would return time and time again. He was also beginning to understand that the enemy had better logistics on their side, and German supplies reaching his forces were becoming a serious issue. By July 1942 he informed Lu that 'my expectations for yesterday's attack were bitterly disappointed. It achieved no success whatever'.[28] A few days later he admitted 'things are going downright badly for me. The enemy is using his superiority, … especially in the infantry to destroy the Italian formations'.

Life was becoming harder, not only on the battlefield but strain was taking its toll, and in August 1942, he told his wife Lu there 'was a lot of sickness…even I am very tired and limp …we've all got heat diarrhoea now'.[29] His mind was not just in Africa but he kept up to date on what was happening elsewhere noting that the Battle for Stalingrad 'seems to be going very hard and is tying up a lot for forces which we could make better use of in the south'; in this he showed a better mind for strategy than the Führer.[30] Later he told Lu that Paulus in Stalingrad 'is perhaps even worse off than I am. He has a more unhuman enemy'.[31] By October 1942 he wrote that it was now a 'very hard struggle, everything is at stake again', a few days later saying it was now in God's hands', which may possibly have been his way of saying that they needed a miracle. So, it was no surprise when later in December 42 he told Lu that 'it would need a miracle for us to hold on much longer'.[32] The rest of his correspondence must have made depressing reading for his wife, because the Germans were now losing, and his health was not good. The Führer sent an order about which Rommel wrote in his diary that 'this order demanded the impossible'.

Although Rommel was now internationally famous as the 'Desert Fox', but North Africa was an allied victory. Rommel was sent to Greece and hardly set his feet on the ground when ordered to Italy where he clashed with Kesselring over strategy, and after a brief time was back in France organising the Channel defences, wounded by an allied aircraft and eliminated after the 20 July Plot. He was a national hero and even respected by the enemy.

In these family letters, mainly to his wife Lu, and a few to his son Manfred, we can see the inner mind of this German general. Not only do we find his love of his family, his sense of optimism and his acceptance of reality, knowing the tide had turned against Nazi Germany. He recognised the logistical strength of the Allies, the power of air control, the loss of supplies in the Mediterranean. We can also read his views on his Italian allies and their lack of fighting ability, and his views on some in the German High Command. He wrote freely about his ups and downs with a sense of honesty he could only share with his wife as he trusted her. For this writer, these personal letters confirm that he was a sound commander, an honest man, and probably most likeable, and it takes Oral History to reveal these views.

HANS-JOACHIM SCHRAEPLER

LIEUTENANT COLONEL ADJUTANT TO ROMMEL 1941

Rommel's adjutant during most of 1941 was Hans-Joachim Schraepler killed in a motor accident in December of the same year, and his letters home were discovered amongst his wife's belongings by their son Hans-Albrecht. They were originally published in French under the title *Mon père, l'aide de camp du Général Rommel*, in 2007, and followed by the English version *At Rommel's Side* in 2009.[33] He had seen action in Poland and France, he was wounded in the latter campaign and impressed Rommel enough to be requested to join his staff in North Africa.

In his letters he mentioned several times about his comrades having their letters returned by the censor's office which always concerned him, but possibly because of his position he managed to successfully post his family letters which were kept by his widow, even though they contained details of the fighting and comments on Rommel. His son Hans-Albrecht took on the task of editing the letters and occasionally providing his own comments and insights. These letters are of interest at several levels, describing the fighting in the North African theatre, his views of Rommel, of their Italian allies, and the English enemy. Perhaps importantly they offer insights into the mindset and conduct of the professional German military officer class. Not long before he died, he mentioned in his diary that he had been recommended for promotion to lieutenant colonel which he heard about on 11 November, and it happened before he died.[34] He wrote to his wife almost on a daily basis, and naturally not all letters probably arrived, but his son noted in the *Foreword* of the book that he found about 400 pages.

In the first correspondence he wrote to his wife from Rome explaining he was about to fly directly to 'Karl', which was the German code word for Rommel, and described Rome to her with its huge buildings full of the 'remnants of ancient Rome everywhere'.[35] Although he was to write about military activities and comment on events all letters were sent to the censor, although today's reader would view these as harmless family letters, there are some elements in his letters over which he was lucky the censor had not returned them. He described flying around Malta 'an English base' and offered his wife a brief picture of his destination in Tripoli full of different races including Germans in their new uniforms. Later he would realise how important the island of Malta was to the battle of the North African deserts, writing that 'Malta probably has to be occupied first, as we cannot leave the English at our flank'.[36] He described how Rommel did not know he had arrived, but was pleased to see him, 'in great joy' as he wrote, and explained all that was happening 'about which' he reminded his wife, 'I cannot tell you'.[37]

He described Rommel as an 'impressive personality 'and in this second letter announced a view he was often to repeat that 'the current difficulties of competence with the Italian troops were removed. They will of course, never stop, Rommel has great plans'.[38] Quite what he was implying in this is difficult to fathom, whether he implied Italian military incompetence was a thing of the past or would always be an issue could be read either way. As his letters unfold it becomes clear in his opinion that it was the second opinion that the Italian soldier was not that reliable. This was confirmed a few days later when Rommel had returned from inspecting some Italian troops and Schraepler wrote 'he did not look satisfied with it, as far as I could tell'.[39] The German military attitude towards the Italians was well-known, and according to many other accounts the British were more concerned about meeting Germans on the battlefield than Italians. It is sheer nonsense and wrong to claim the Italians were cowards, the reasons can be found elsewhere. Many Italians had never wanted the war in the first place, many had families in Britain and America, Mussolini's demand for restoring the Roman Empire did not appeal to every Italian citizen, and like many others the soldiers must have asked themselves why they were expected to die for a mere sand-dune. The other factor can be located in what Schraepler believed to being led by poor officers. He informed his wife when he had been invited to the Italian mess for lunch, noting that 'the Italian officers live very well, while the ordinary ranks have to be content with lesser fare, with bread and canned meat and red wine'.[40] This would have been the same for British troops but more tea than red wine, and the other factors were to do with such elements as the Germans had their proud Prussian military tradition, the British were fighting for survival, and later in the war when Italian partisans were fighting for the same reason their courage was often noted. He noted later that the Italian officers had better 'tents, field chairs and a kitchen is so incomparably more luxurious than ours'.[41] On one occasion when

Germans and Italians were attacking Fortress Medannar they were met with dense artillery fire, and when the Italians wanted to withdraw he told his wife that he insulted them, swore at them and drew his pistol 'and they did what I told them and they began to dig in'.[42]

His life in Africa started with long plane and road journeys with Rommel inspecting his widespread troops, but often as the months passed by Rommel would leave Schraepler at the base to sort out administration work while he did his tours. Schraepler described that on his arrival they were being bombed by the English (as with most Germans of this period, he always used the term 'English' as opposed to 'British') which was to dominate many of his letters during the year. As his months in the desert passed, he was constantly referring to the bombing raids, occasionally rejoicing when an enemy plane was brought down, but it is clear that although at this time the Germans and Italians had strength on the ground, they did not have the same asset in the air-war. He was even concerned that Rommel at times did not have enough sleep because of the continuous bombing.[43] Near the end of the year he became Crüwell's adjutant, and he preferred the new man because Rommel only called Schraepler when he had orders to give, and the staff felt better with the new man, 'but the new general demands far more attention than Rommel. That takes much time'.[44]

One of the major issues faced by the *Afrika Korps* was receiving insufficient supplies mentioned early in the letters in February, his first month there. As he occasionally relates this problem, he naturally tends to blame the Italians, but he does not mention the domination of the Mediterranean by the British, but on one occasion questions why the Germans had not taken Gibraltar to 'close the gateway'. He referred later to the German attack on Russia (Operation *Barbarossa*), enthusiastic about success without realising that the Eastern war was placing North Africa into a minor role which would also influence supplies, although he had noted that 'the *Afrika Korps* only gets what Berlin reserve for us, and we have to accept it'.[45] Time and time again they struggled even for the basic resources of petrol and water.[46] He was also concerned that the British seemed to 'have a huge stock of ammunition' because they had the upper hand at sea and in the air.[47] Later in the year even food supplies were seriously diminished, especially, as he noted, when 'we finished our reserves from the English booty'.[48]

The Germans were at this stage making progress, and Schraepler noted that 'we advance with great speed. The English are withdrawing, although they fight very bravely'.[49] It was clear he had some respect for British troops later noting they were defending Tobruk 'with tenacity'.[50] He also wrote that they 'could be mean', referring to a time an English soldier called them in German to move forward, which they did and were shot or captured.[51] He seemed to forget that in war when men are fighting to stay alive it is not a gentleman's game of chess. Nevertheless, he raised the pertinent point that there is always a vicious streak in any war, and he pointed out that the 'English have systematically bombed German military hospitals'.[52]

On the brighter side he described a visit by the Italian General Gariboldi who presented Rommel with a 'brand new caravan with sofa, folding bed, table, two cabinets, toilet, shower, electric light and water pump'.[53] Through most of his time with Rommel, Schraepler appeared to admire Rommel, writing to his wife in March that 'I have never met anyone until now as agile in thinking and acting as him. He is full engaged by the fulfilment of his mandate, and he sets an example rarely encountered'.[54]

He mentions the nature of the conflict, many times, often finding himself close to the frontline, and wounded. He suffered as many others mention, from the excessive heat and informing his wife he was suffering from a 'plethora of sand fleas, very small animals that you can only feel when, full of blood and the size of small peas, they abandon your body leaving fierce itching'.[55] He informed his wife that the Führer had told Rommel to stop putting so much effort in taking Tobruk and carry out smaller attacks elsewhere, and it was surprising this letter passed the censor.[56] As Rommel's adjutant he had to spend time on answering letters of admiration sent to Rommel by youngsters and adults of both sexes.[57]

As with his chief Rommel, Schraepler was curious about events happening elsewhere, the attack on Crete and the war against the Soviet Union. He only ever heard the good news because of his early death, writing to his wife 'it's marvellous. I regret not being on the expedition. This campaign must be joyful and refreshing'.[58] It would have seemed better to avoid the sandflies and heat of the North African deserts, but at this stage the Russian winter had not yet arrived with its bitter ferocity, and with the benefit of hindsight he was not personally to know that compared to the Eastern war, the battles in North Africa were relatively clean and almost gentlemanly compared to the Soviet conflict.

Near the end of his life one of his letters records a bemusing note about a very lucky General Müller-Gebhard whose car was blown up and yet he survived. When removing his gear from the wrecked car he found in the passenger's well a dangerous but dead three-foot snake. The same general missed his plane flight, only to hear that was also lucky because the plane crashed with no survivors.[59] As a matter of interest General Müller-Gebhard was lucky because he survived to 80, dying in 1970.

These letters are family letters but are the views of a senior German officer working under Rommel. Rommel appears in a good light and as a very individual personality, but his successor Crüwell comes out in slightly better colours for his officers. Either way it is clear the Germans had good professional commanders. He constantly refers to the lack of fighting quality of the Italian military, hinting, probably correctly that it had much to do with the officer class. He appeared in his letters to have a respect for the 'English' [British] opposition, twice accusing them of unnecessary cruelty, but he died too early to hear of the Nazi barbarities exposed in the Nuremberg trials. He was aware of the Royal Air Force power, not least because of the constant bombing he mentions, which kept Rommel awake and made him moody in the early mornings, but also the lack of supplies for which he heaped some blame on the Italians, forgetting the British had a better control of the Mediterranean, causing him to think that occupying Malta and Gibraltar would help. There is nothing startling in his letters, except it allows us inside the mindset of what appears to be a civilised senior German officer who was there in North Africa until his death.

GEORGE PATTON LETTERS
TOP COMMANDER OR EGOTIST

The Man Patton

George Patton, a well-known American General was often regarded by the Germans as the best leader on the Allied side. His own superiors realised, as with the German opinion, that he could win battles with his intense ambition to succeed. He saw action in North Africa, Sicily, and then in Western Europe. He was so ambitious he believed he was a man of destiny. Prior to landing in Africa one biographer D'Este quoted him as stating that he felt the responsibility like a 'ton of bricks', but 'I am not in the least worried. I can't decide logically if I am a man of destiny or a lucky fool, but I think I am destined'.[60]

His reputation was frequently marred by his personal conduct for which at one time he was sidelined. His nickname was 'Old Blood and Guts', and it was known that his speeches to the men before battle were barbarically incitive and foulmouthed. He spent time in his usual robust fashion addressing the troops before they set sail, warning of surrender tricks, killing snipers and 'all Germans', and just before they left, he warned that 'in landing operations, retreat is impossible. To surrender is as ignoble as it is foolish'.[61] His main concern was the navy which he considered the weak spot, 'which was a misjudgement', but he was always critical of others.[62] He needed to be seen as the prime figure on the stage. It has been claimed that before entering Messina,

Patton instructed Truscott to wait for his arrival so he could make the entry, for which Bradley was furious. The historian Douglas Porch wrote that 'Patton had emerged as the hero of Operation *Husky*. But in the process, his legendary cavalryman's audacity had passed over into recklessness and lack of self-control'.[63]

He was like Mark Clark, deeply Anglophobic and his dislike of Montgomery was well-known. For many observers he was either adored or disliked, with some historians more scathing than others, with another historian, Gerhard Weinberg describing him as 'an egomaniac'.[64] There is no doubt, as can be seen in his letters, he was a man driven by raging ambition.

No one could doubt his military leadership qualities in stirring men up to fight, but it was his personal behaviour which brought down heavy criticism even from his supporters such as Eisenhower. There were two known incidents when two of his men shot Italian prisoners of war for no reason while in Sicily. A chaplain came across their bodies, Omar Bradley was made aware, and two war correspondents also heard about the massacres. In his diary of 14 July Patton explained how he told Bradley 'That it was probably an exaggeration, but in any case, to tell the officer to certify that the dead men were snipers or had attempted to escape'.[65] The men were eventually punished but in a very moderate way.

Patton was well known to visit his men in hospital, on one occasion at the 15th Evacuation Hospital, he met Private Charles Kuhl (who had malaria, chronic diarrhoea, and high fever) whom Patton slapped with folded gloves calling him a coward. Kuhl had no obvious wounds for Patton to see, and he assumed he was a coward. Kuhl was evacuated to North Africa to recover and later landed in Normandy in 1944. A similar incident occurred at another Evacuation Hospital with Private Paul Bennett. Patton was furious as he said, 'it makes my blood boil to think of a yellow bastard being babied' and waved his pistol in his face.[66] Patton was now in disgrace because he was behaving like the hated image of an over-zealous Nazi officer and was sent back to Britain. Even in this environment he often blundered with his public remarks and comments, the most infamous being dubbed the 'Knutsford incident'. This was an address to a public gathering, when Patton mentioned the Soviets, explaining that after the war it would be 'Anglo-American domination'. It was reported, and the newspaper article caused a major embarrassment with George Marshall leaving the embarrassment to an angry Eisenhower, who felt like sacking Patton, with Bradley agreeing. However, Churchill and Eisenhower needed fighting commanders, and Patton survived. From a young man he had this projected sense of personal destiny and was convinced he was always right, but 'there were occasions when it could and did get him into trouble'.[67] As early as 1928 senior officers had noted down in their reports that Patton 'would be invaluable in time of war but a disturbing element in time of peace'.[68]

He was initially used by the High Command to lead a 'fake army' in East Anglia to convince the Germans the landings would be in the Pas de Calais which along with other diversions managed to work, and he led the Third Army into Europe. He lived up to expectations and his war record was good, not only in the post D-Day Normandy battles, but his incisive thrusts into enemy territory. He was so successful on many occasions that it caused many German commanders to regard him as the best of all commanders.

His letters to his wife Beatrice when he was in North Africa had expressed concern about their son-in-law Colonel John Waters. As early as 23 February 1943 he had written 'John's battalion was practically wiped out, but he is thought to be safe', but later he discovered he was in a German PoW camp.[69] He had been captured by the Germans, and Patton had been informed that his relation was in Hammelburg (Oflag XIII-B). Patton, when in that area, sent a task force into enemy held territory which was a disaster and all but a few of the 300 men sent were not killed, wounded, or captured and it achieved nothing.* Patton had ordered Captain Abraham Baum to penetrate fifty miles of

---

* Only 15 survived without injury or capture according to Kershaw, Alex, *The Liberator* (London: Hutchinson, 2012), p.236.

enemy territory with some sixteen tanks, nearly thirty half-tracks and approximately 300 men. They did not have the appropriate maps and no location of the prison camp, which was by any estimation a foolhardy thing to do, and immoral as it caused many unnecessary deaths.

Patton's reputation was again sullied and one historian and World War veteran Dwight Macdonald called Patton 'a swaggering bigmouth, a Fascist-minded aristocrat…brutal and hysterical, coarse, and affected, violent and empty…compared to the dreary run of us, General Patton was quite mad'.[70] As is well-known, Patton died in a car accident which for some who were worried about the postwar years was a relief.

Some postwar historians still agree with Macdonald; others look to the better side of his powerful leadership and his victories. It is a conundrum which has often fixated this writer, and when the book *The Patton Papers* was published, it contained many personal letters which provide some clues.[71] The next brief part will refer to a mere few to demonstrate the way personal letters offer insights into a person's mind and thinking patterns.

The Patton Papers

These published papers run to nearly 900 pages and are packed with Patton's diary, his own letters and those received from his wife Beatrice, others to and from other commanders, politicians and many others. They follow the date line of his very full diary, but it is the letters which have much to say in terms of Oral History, though the diary can also be more than useful. The warning from the editor Blumenson must always be kept in mind when he wrote 'the diary entries are occasionally self-serving, sometimes inaccurate, always perceptive and fresh', which is why this study has ignored the diary and looked to the personal letters.[72]

He was a complex character, impulsive, ambitious, demanding, religious in his own way, self-seeking, and highly critical of others. In an early letter to an Aunt Susie, he wrote 'you must see the wonderful, good effect your careful assistance to my upbringing has produced, knowing that you have a great drag [influence] with the Lord. I trust you will bring all your efforts to prayerful intercession that I may soon get another star and be a lieutenant general. When that comes you can keep right on working for four stars for me'.[73] The reader can feel his ambition and expectation that the 'Lord' is looking after his military career.

His often self-proclaimed spirit for fighting was encouraged by others which can be seen in a letter sent to him by Lieutenant Commander Eller commending his fighting spirit as the Allies 'greatest need is for effective aggressive leadership', quoting a newspaper article referring to him as 'you win war with guts not machines'. Patton always saw his role as preparing men for fighting with outright aggression.

In August 1942 he was in London, in which in a letter to his wife he described it as 'a dead city' with just military cars and a few taxis. He wrote 'I am treated with great reverence as a prospective hero…and so far, as I can see, the generals are about my age but less well preserved'. It may have appeared less conceited if he used the word hope or friendship instead of 'reverence', which intimated they worshipped him.

As he was heading for Africa (Operation *Torch*) in November 1942 he informed his wife of the rumour that the French [Vichy] might join them against the Germans, adding 'I hope not, for it would sort of pull the cork out of the men – all steamed up to fight…also it would be better for me to have a battle'.[74] This indicated an almost juvenile approach wanting his gang to win a playground fight. He missed the political ramifications of Vichy-France as well as the military consequences had they changed sides. For him this intimated that organising his men to fight to the death was all that counted. His mixed-up thinking can be seen in a letter he wrote to Secretary of War Henry Stimson in December 1942 that 'we had a fairly hard fight and lost some good men, but we inflicted very severe casualties on our late enemies [the French] …of course as a Christian I was very glad to avoid further fusion of blood, but as a soldier I would have given a good deal to have the fight go on'.[75] He went on to describe how he treated the surrendered French leaders by commending their gallantry, looking to 'end the fratricidal strife' and resume the age-old friendship between France and the USA, spending $40 dollars to treat the meeting with champagne. It was a lengthy letter as he tried to show the Secretary for War what a good soldier he was, and also a sound diplomat. Again, he appeared to neglect that occupied France was still fighting under de Gaulle's Free French, who saw the Americans as allies.

He was constantly selling himself. To his wife Beatrice in November 1942 he wrote that 'unfortunately I did not get a chance to distinguish myself during the fighting except to not lay down a couple of times when we got strafed'.[76] Any good commander would not do this, as a person in a high position should set an example by at least showing common sense and it would do his men little good if he were killed.

He was annoyed when he heard Mark Clark had been given the Medal of Honour for 'riding on a submarine'.[77] He belittled himself with this statement and the event, but it was a dangerous role Clark had played as he was entering potential enemy territory for secret talks. Later he was just as angry with Clark, telling Beatrice 'The Fifth Army under Clark…makes me mad but there is nothing that can be done about it'.[78]

His own self-importance is always at the fore of much of his correspondence informing Beatrice in late December 1942 that 'I am going to a nearby country next week to talk to a potentate. I was specially selected by the W. D. [War Department] due to "my demonstrated tact and personality"'.[79] He wrote that some people seem to have changed 'their ideas about him?' He knew that his reputation was being outspoken, critical, and often impulsive. Perhaps his account of giving the French Vichy commanders some champagne had recoloured views.

These selected examples come from the first 141 pages of the book, and they disclose much about Patton's personality. Some of the letters to Beatrice clearly indicate they were working as a pair on his reputation, she was watching and reading the press reports and building up his image. As the first part of this section tried to make clear, he was seen as a necessarily aggressive commander, even his supporters such as Eisenhower knew he had flaws, but the extracted letters, a few mentioned above take us deep into his mindset, his love of war, his ambitious drive, his jealousy of others, and it is up to the reader of these letters to determine whether Patton was an excellent commander of men at war, or just an egotist of gigantic proportions.

GEORGE ORWELL

LETTERS

The famous writer George Orwell was born in 1903, and his real name was Eric Arthur Blair. He was an outstanding intellectual famous for many works including *Animal Farm* and the dystopian novel *Nineteen Eighty-Four*, and many other works. He was known for his socialist style criticism, his opposition to any form of autocracy, be it dictatorship or totalitarianism or any other form. He was a dedicated democratic socialist, and he fought against Franco in the Spanish Civil War. He was shot through the throat, repaired, but he was unfit for fighting, and was turned down by the military when the Second World War started. He had many books, articles and papers published and is still widely read. He kept a daily diary which has some interesting insights in between his noting the weather changes every day and how his vegetable garden was doing – this was published in 2011, 61 years after his death.[80] A year later the same editor published all his letters written over his short lifetime.[81] Orwell was a man obsessed with pen and paper or a typewriter, his professional work as a journalist, his publications are simply immense, and in addition to this he was a prolific diary keeper and letter writer. The published books come in painfully small font. This will be a brief exposure of a few of his comments in his letters during the war years which relate to his thinking of war life and what was happening around him.

In 8 January 1940 in a letter to his first publisher Victor Gollancz, he explained that he could not send him a book because the police had been and seized all his books which had come by post. 'The police', he wrote, 'were only carrying out orders and were very nice about it'.[82] He explained the public prosecutor had written that his need for books was understandable. This reflected the war years where suspicion was rife, and because of his years abroad he may have been more carefully noted. In the same letter he expressed his inner belief when he wrote 'what worries me at the present is the uncertainty as to whether the ordinary people in countries like England grasp the difference between democracy and despotism well enough to want to defend their liberties'. He would have been conscious of the occasional popularity during the 1930s of the would-be autocrat Oswald Mosley; there were those who had supported Franco, admirers of Mussolini, and until a few months before September 1939 even some who thought Hitler was doing well. In April 1940, he wrote to Geoffry Gorer a social anthropologist noting that he had failed to find war work, writing that 'now we are in this bloody war we have got to win it, and I would like to lend a hand'.[83] He even explained he wanted to lay off writing for a time, which would have been difficult for a man like him. He had been turned down because of his Spanish Civil War injury and problems with his lungs, and on the administration side there may have been some doubt because he was by now a well-known left-wing socialist.

On 22 June 1940 he wrote to the editor of *Time and Tide* explaining that England would probably be invaded soon and 'our slogan should be ARM THE PEOPLE.' He admitted he was no competent military leader but the war in France and Spain had offered some clear facts. 'One is that when the civil population is unarmed, parachutists, motor cyclists, and stray tanks can not only work fearful havoc but draw off large bodies of regular troops…the advantages of arming the population outweigh the danger of putting weapons into the wrong hands'.[84] The rest of the letter, intended as an article, went on to describe what would later be called Partisan war. He was basing much of this on his experience in Spain. He was basically saying that the government had to trust the people. There were some preparations taking place in the event of a successful German invasion, and to this day people would have divided opinions about arming the population. In medieval England every peasant was expected to practice at the butts with their bows, and all expected to fight. In France some of the hitherto unruly and unsocial teenagers became the best resistance fighters. It is a complex issue, but at least Orwell had the courage to voice his views. He joined the Local Defence Volunteers (later called the Home Guard) and his experience in Spain proved useful in how to react to an incursion by enemy troops.

There were occasions when in his public writings he made mistakes. He had tended to follow the French wish or myth that the best tank theories arose from de Gaulle and was criticised by B.H. Liddell Hart, (then a captain). There had been considerable discussion about tanks in warfare (with which Liddell-Hart had been involved) with mixed reactions from various military men. The Germans had watched and listened but under von Seeckt during the interbellum years had experimented with the use of lorries dressed up as tanks combined with infantry and possible air support for their use in what has since been dubbed Blitzkrieg war. Orwell was quick to apologise to Liddell-Hart, and he did so readily and openly. He would have been aware that de Gaulle was not a popular person with the British and later the Americans. Orwell had experienced firsthand fighting, but he admitted he was no expert, writing to Liddell-Hart 'I am sorry I accepted too readily the legend of the Germans having taken their tank theories from de Gaulle'.[85] He explained that although it was a 'misfortune that we didn't succeed in getting a leftwing politician of some standing out of France, but since de Gaulle is the only figure we have at present to represent the Free French we must make the best of him'.[86] Orwell was constantly doing his best in the war effort and his steering wheel was his political viewpoint.

In late 1942 he wrote to the editor of *The Times*. His main concern was as a consequence of the Dieppe Raid when Canadian commandos had tied up German prisoners, the Germans had retaliated by chaining their British PoWS and the British were counter-threatening. Orwell wrote that by doing this 'we descend, at any rate in the eyes of the ordinary observer to the level of our enemies…there is a deep moral difference between a democracy and fascism…the fascist principle is two eyes for an eye and a whole set of teeth for one tooth'.[87] Orwell was making the important point that the British were civilised people unlike fascists, and although his critics saw him as a left-wing intellectual, he was, because of his moral understanding of the value of democracy, worth hearing.

Most of his diary is very personal, about his family, the various jobs he held, with publishers and editors of newspapers and magazines. However, he is still regarded as one the great intellectuals of his time, well known for his hatred of fascists and any form of dictatorship, he was ready to die for his democratic country, was nearly killed when fighting against Franco, and while his letters are very personal, they are worth reading. They come from an astute and intelligent man who recorded everything nearly every day, from the weather and garden to major events and their ramifications and should be seen as sound Oral History.

Chapter Three

Diaries are Time Capsules

INTRODUCTION

From children to leading world figures, diaries are often kept not just as a source of information for later reading and reminiscence, but to reflect on events in their own lives. Most diaries are only of personal interest and for family consumption, because they are often deeply personal. However, if the diarist has an important role and their integrity is deemed reliable, they become an intriguing source of interest to historians, and for all those who wonder what really happened in the past. Ordinary frontline soldiers may have kept logbooks, but the real interest focuses on those who had the time and space to not only write what happened, but to comment on the events of their day. Occasionally the diary is written from a sense of self-discipline, as a record of events and decisions or knowing that one day it may be read for information which makes it more like a 'time capsule', and therefore an invaluable part of Oral History. There are historically some famous and well-known diarists such as Samuel Pepys with national and personal notes, and Anne Frank's diary portraying the horrors of the Nazi regime.

Family diarists are only of interest to families, though researchers of social history often find them useful. Individuals keep diaries for a variety of reasons, one colleague telling this writer she did it to link with future generations, which amounted to her version of a time capsule. John Colville, a senior civil servant during the Second World War wrote 'I believe historians, if they try to throw themselves back into the conditions in which decisions were taken', may find a different perspective.[1] Personal diaries often provide not only new information but invaluable insights.

Historians often rely on passing their opinions or judgments based on research and hindsight, but a diary can often challenge this and provide a more realistic appraisal, because a diary can take us back in time and provide a realistic guide. Some diaries written by 'people in the know' not only reveal much about the nature of the diarist (important if they were in a leading role) but why the decisions of the day were taken, and the consequences. Other more personal diaries give a different perspective about the emotions and feelings of the day.

The driving force and motivations of those diarists who were associated with the major leaders reveals much not only about the relevant diarist, but about the leaders and their regimes or governments, which is a sound form of Oral History. Naturally there are some diaries which have to be checked first to ensure there were no later additions often to justify past actions, and some were kept as preparation for autobiography, and in some countries, they were banned if the author was working at a senior level. In Britain during the Second World War anyone in the service of the government was not supposed to keep diaries for security reasons. However, this did not stop the above-mentioned John Colville who was Churchill's Secretary, nor Alan Lascelles the King's Secretary. There were many others including Field Marshal Alan Brooke, Lord Mountbatten, Lieutenant Generals Pownall and Wavell, Harold Macmillan and Anthony Eden, with many others. Many of these diaries have been published at various times, there are others now in family libraries and archives, and all offer insights not only into the nature of their writers, but into the history of their times. Many of these diarists knew that keeping a diary was not generally acceptable because of their position, especially Lascelles working for the King, and Colville at 10 Downing Street who wrote about the time Churchill demanded the need for keeping matters secret, about which he wrote that 'this suddenly makes me feel rather conscious-stricken about this diary. I haven't the heart to destroy it and shall compromise by keeping its locked up here, even more strictly than hitherto'.[2]

The nine diaries selected here come from British, German, Italian and Russian sources, ranging from highly significant figures to a White Russian émigrée and a persecuted German Jew.

FIELD MARSHAL LORD ALAN BROOKE
CHIEF OF IMPERIAL GENERAL STAFF

One diary which is outstandingly interesting is that of Alan Brooke who during the critical years of the Second World War was the Imperial Chief of the General Staff and was in constant touch with Winston Churchill.[3] It appeared that he wrote this diary mainly for the benefit of his wife Benita, and although it contained political and military information, he often used the Royal Mail, even though he was a known martinet on security. After the war during 1957 and later in 1959 Sir Arthur Bryant published sections of Brooke's diaries in the books *The Turn of the Tide* and *Triumph in the West*. The first publication in 1957 caused 'a considerable stir…because it portrayed the irritations as well as the glories that fell to those who worked under Sir Winston Churchill in the direction of the war', because Bryant had liberally edited chosen passages causing a degree of controversy at the time.[4]

When it appeared in public, the diary presented the figure of Alan Brooke as a military leader always critical of others, especially Churchill. When the *Sunday Times* in 1957 produced a lurid and controversial series, based on Bryant's input, it produced only a mild response from Churchill, who was against diaries written under the stress of war. Bryant's incursions had not always been reliable and in places were misleading. When the diaries are read today it is clear that Brooke was a deeply emotional man who shared his anxieties with his wife. He admits to her his mistakes, his pent-up anger and his many frustrations, especially with Churchill and some other leading figures, not just his own countrymen. He described the French leader de Gaulle in his diary as 'a horrible specimen', and he was equally critical of some leading American military such as Eisenhower and George Marshall. It was not all clashes and vitriol, because the photographs of Brooke as a grim horn-rimmed bespectacled man ignored the wider image of him enjoying humorous moments, with Kennedy noting that 'Brooke had a great sense of humour and his descriptions of meetings with Winston are very good fun'.[5]

The diaries also reveal below his so-called stern puritanical features a highly sensitive man. He loved his wife, and when his predecessor Field Marshal John Dill died in America, he was given a statue in Arlington cemetery but never received in Britain a peerage for which Brooke blamed Churchill. Brooke visited his wounded son Tom at the front, and when his ADC Barney was killed in an aircraft accident he was struck with sheer grief. He may have had the nickname of Colonel Shrapnel in the War Office, but the diary paints a picture of a man who cared for his friends and neighbours.[6]

Of paramount interest for the public was the strange relationship between Brooke and the much-adored Churchill. When Brooke was asked to take over the top position he hesitated, not because of serving Churchill, but he wondered about leaving his present post on the domestic Home Forces for the global scene, writing that 'the consequences of failures or mistakes are a nightmare to think about'.[7] Brooke's task was twofold, first he had to look at the grand strategy on a global basis, and secondly, keep a watching brief over the army and its expansion, after its major reduction in size during the interbellum years.

Throughout this diary Brooke was acutely aware and knowledgeable of the global war, involved in discussions about the air war and the issues relating to strategic as compared to tactical bombing. He was part of the discussions on naval strategy and conducted army interests. He travelled the world, worked with the Americans, met Stalin, was awarded a Soviet medal, travelled to North Africa, and was involved with the Japanese War. Reading his diaries is like having a first-hand tour of the Second World War in an oral history lesson because most of his diary is day by day, not recollections but as it happened.

He was truthful in his diary entries, a classic example being his attitude to Admiral of the Fleet Sir Dudley Pound, about whom his early diary entries were quite damming and cynical. Brooke appeared never to lose his basic humanity and felt angry with himself and sad when he later discovered Pound was seriously ill and dying. The diary clearly shows the stress and strain of high command during these difficult years.

A revealing aspect of the diaries was the relationship between the democratic leadership of an elected prime minister and the military leaders, a vexed area which never concerned any form of autocratic leadership such as Hitler. When Churchill was angry with Auchinleck, he had drafted a critical letter to the general full of abuse, but Brooke and his colleagues managed to moderate the message before it was sent. The relationship between a government and the military leadership in times of war or stress is an important feature in any democracy. The elected government is the leading head of all decisions by the principles of democracy, and in military matters this can lead to problems when the military experts feel political amateurs were ordering them to a catastrophe. Churchill was often open to their criticism, as he was in America where they had not forgotten Churchill's Gallipoli disaster and wondered why Churchill wanted to fight in North African deserts, some thinking that the preservation of the British Empire was his only motive. The Americans wanted to cross the channel into occupied France as soon as possible. Churchill and Brooke were united on this issue, and they agreed that the highly professional Germany military would repulse such a move if it were done too hurriedly. It was Brooke who travelled to America to point this out. Some Americans disliked his way of lecturing them but recognised his authority and experience. The American General Omar Bradley later in his memoirs admitted after the Americans had fought Rommel in North Africa that Brooke had been correct in his views, writing 'I came to the conclusion that it was fortunate that the British view prevailed, that the US Army first met the enemy on the periphery, in Africa rather than on the beaches of France. In Africa we learnt to crawl, to walk and then run. Had that learning process been launched in France it would surely have, as Alan Brooke argued, resulted in an unthinkable disaster'.[8]

Brooke's powerful and often justified criticism of colleagues caused a stir when the diaries were first published, but controversy ensued when he wrote about his clashes and views with the almost worshipped Churchill.

There were times when Brooke in his diary admitted he was angry, even wishing the Prime Minister would die before he tarnished his reputation, or claiming he had an 'unbalanced mind'. General Pug Ismay who liked both men noted in his memoirs that both were exhausted. It was a two-way relationship, and both Churchill and Brooke were constantly blunt with one another on many occasions. On more than one occasion Brooke wondered whether he would be dismissed, but Churchill, being Churchill, deliberately chose strong people even if they challenged him. However, Churchill was always unhappy when in conflict with his military advisers or with the Americans, 'but when he had to make a choice between them, he came down firmly on Brooke's side'.[9]

Brooke told many amusing stories about Churchill, how he could be like a spoilt child and trying to take away 'from him a dangerous toy, [by which he meant some dangerous idea] it could take days or weeks!'[10] There were many contentious conflicts with Churchill, but there were amusing moments, and laughter. Brooke often quoted some of Churchill's lines because of their amusement or literary succinctness, and even in heated discussions others found their exchanges amusing. Churchill once complained about all the accessories the army required, he compared the service to a Peacock with an unnecessarily massive tail, to which the keen ornithologist Brooke promptly retorted that without its tail the Peacock would lose balance. Despite the general impression it was not always friction, there were good times.

When Brooke's diary was first published, Churchill was annoyed and the tension of the war years continued into the postwar era. In Churchill's visitors' book kept at Chartwell there is a list of signed visitors with many being regular, Montgomery appears some forty-six times, frequently Alexander, but there is not a single entry for Brooke.[11] Colville later noted that 'Brooke was the only man on whom I ever saw him [Churchill] deliberately and ostentatiously turn his back'.[12] This postwar time was much sadder than all the internal conflict of the war years. Despite the argumentative challenges between Brooke and Churchill, the prime minister always supported Brooke and nearly always took his advice. In Brooke's case despite his occasional vitriolic outbursts, he not only admired Churchill but liked him.

The most important element of Brooke's diary is that it was a daily diary written as events occurred, and his comments told the truth about Brooke's feelings and major events and issues during the war years. It was as close to good oral history as could be hoped, and it faithfully portrays the tensions and mixed points of view, as well as the different personalities involved in the top command.

GALEAZZO CIANO

MUSSOLINI'S FOREIGN MINISTER AND SON-IN-LAW

Ciano was Mussolini's son-in-law having married his daughter Edda, and became his foreign minister, and through his diary-keeping has left many insights from the Italian perspective during the Second World War and the preceding years. Ciano was described by one of Mussolini's biographers as 'vain, pompous, frivolous, hedonistic, a snob and devoid of any fixed belief'.[13] Ciano's diaries reveal almost Machiavellian diplomatic habits, noting both his rise and fall from power, gaining an insight of these years through his critical meetings with heads of state, and the political machinations which preceded the war. Mussolini surrounded himself with selected henchmen and after his marriage to Mussolini's daughter Edda, Ciano's rise to fame was meteoric as was his fall from power. At the personal level of Ciano's life, he was a spoilt child from the upper classes of Italian society, developing into a playboy with a dubious reputation as a profligate womaniser. Ciano and Edda had what is best described as 'an open marriage', and they were often at odds with one another, but she stayed loyal to him to the end, namely his execution by her father's regime.

Ciano started as the propaganda minister, launching press attacks about the international condemnation of the campaign in Abyssinia. This drew the attention of Anthony Eden, the British Foreign Secretary (1935-38), who later wrote 'the fact that Count Ciano was the Minister of Propaganda encouraged this activity, his object being to add to his own authority'. He also trained as a pilot. However, politics was more attractive, and he was confident in the support of Mussolini, his father-in-law, 'he was eager to show his independence of the wiser counsels of the Italian Foreign Office'.[14] When in 1936 Mussolini sent his then Foreign Minister Dino Grandi to London as ambassador, Ciano took his place after Mussolini had assumed the role for a brief time. This step up the political ladder meant Ciano would meet the leading figures on the European stage, and he travelled widely; this alone makes his diary observations interesting as his insights are of some curiosity as they change over time.

His Diary

Ciano's diaries must be treated with caution, he was aware that keeping his diaries was public knowledge, including Mussolini who asked about them, and later they were much sought after by the Germans and the Americans. Many histories of Italy during this era frequently have disparaging views, but like him or hate him, Ciano as a leading Italian makes for informative reading, and his life and views broadens the historical perspectives with some penetrating insights. Ciano's written diaries were mere calendar notebooks used by the Italian Red Cross which meant cramped calligraphy. For many historians and experts, they feel that parts have redactions, probably when he was sidelined as ambassador to the Vatican. This is probably the case that he may have experimented with redactions, but they appear as a systematic record. Later he wrote his reflections might be 'sufficient not only to protect me from all political vengeance and persecution but will rehabilitate me even in the eyes of my adversaries.'[15] Even some of the identified redactions remain of interest, as he was executed before the war was over, the redactions when identified can explain his thinking at the time they were written.

This redaction issue has been common with many diarists, and there is a chance that Field Marshal Alan Brooke may have wished he had done so. Some diaries are fake such as the forged Hitler Diaries sold for millions, authenticated for a brief time by Hugh Trevor-Roper. Mussolini was also the centre of fake diaries purchased by a gullible British press. There has been a long debate as to the reliability of Ciano's diaries, but their authenticity has been supported by many who knew him. Mario Toscano wrote in 1948 in the *Rivista Storica Italiana* that, apart from a few remarks, one must recognize in the diary of Ciano one of the most important sources for the history of Fascist foreign policy. One thing is certain, it was not a total redaction, but more like the 'curate's egg' – good or safe in parts.

Ciano's work

The year he was appointed foreign minister in 1936 was a time of frantic diplomatic activity, as there was the Spanish Civil war with Italy supporting Franco, and Mussolini being widely condemned for the occupation of Abyssinia. The Nazi regime was causing concern, and the French and British ambassadors were keen to know if it were true that Italy appeared to be drawing close to Germany, as they did their best to thwart this potential problem. Ciano's diary reflects the intrigue and Machiavellian dancing he played between the French, British and German ambassadors. Hitler had admired Mussolini who in return was less certain about his admirer but his ideas of restoring Roman grandeur was pushing him in Germany's direction, and both dictators hated communist Russia. This meant that Ciano visited Germany and met the leading men many times. The new Germany did not impress Ciano, but he played his cards and said all the right things in the right places. He did, from the earliest stages, long before the suspected redactions happened develop an intense disliking for Ribbentrop. The Germans, looking for a political and military partner welcomed him and Edda with open arms. It was less so in Austria. During these pre-war years the diary conveys the feeling that Ciano was assuming a self-importance on the national scene with so many nations such as Germany, Britain, France, and Spain pandering for his support. It was not just Germany that attracted their attention, but Italy's intentions in the Balkans. The foreign diplomats were never certain because Ciano appeared to vacillate on all the areas of concern, but then diplomats would be accustomed to this approach. Ciano had his eyes on Albania, eventually turning it into a client state and was later blamed for starting the Greek war from which the Germans later rescued Italy. For some he was seen as the 'bully-boy' of the Balkans. He had to deal with the British whose ships they had attacked near Spain and later when the British placed an embargo of Italy's much needed coal supplies. By 1937 following another trip to Germany with Mussolini the diaries make it clear that Ciano's feeling towards the Nazi regime was wavering. He knew both fascist states had different national formulas, Germany's based on 'racism', and Italy on 'Roman Imperialism'. His feelings towards the Nazi regime varied and there was a growing tendency for the Germans to see him just as a social dilettante with changing views.

In Rome he continued his diplomatic dance with the British and French who were trying to woo Italy away from Germany, by avoiding answering questions, being elusive, and sometimes telling lies. When Hitler visited Germany he entered some amusing notes about the German leader, whether they were true or not is another question. Not long after this visit Ciano wrote in his diary that Mussolini 'speaks of going to war left, right and centre, without a clear opponent or a defined objective', sometimes it is Russia, but then he fulminates against France and Britain and even America 'before he calms down.'[16] Ciano continued at every opportunity to enjoy the life of the playboy, but it is easy to gather he was not happy about the prospect of war. He knew Mussolini was slowly leaning in that direction, and so when he met the American representative, he placated the situation by simple double-dealing. Ciano liked to be seen as important, and at the Munich Conference he was pleased the Germans gave him and Mussolini a warmer welcome than anyone else. He would have known that he had some international standing, with his picture appearing on the magazine cover of the American journal *Newsweek* on the same day as Pope Pius XII was enthroned in the Vatican. He was bemused by Chamberlain on his visit to Rome, especially by the news that Chamberlain had no idea how many Jews lived in Britain. However, the Germans were rapidly becoming suspicious of Ciano, having noted that he tended to like the British. Himmler and Reinhard Heydrich had a night-club type venue (called Salon Kitty) to encourage foreign diplomats to attend and record their private conversations. The SS officer Walter Schellenberg claimed postwar that one of the 'biggest catches was the Italian Foreign Minister Count Ciano, who went there with other important diplomats'.[17]

The Second World War through Italian Eyes

Ciano and others knew that Mussolini was veering towards the Nazi regime, with Mussolini telling Ciano that 'governments are like people and must follow a line of morality and honour', which was an odd thing to say as he was intent on entering a major aggressive war, and which portrays much about Mussolini's mindset.[18] When the war started with Mussolini joining in when the German victory over France was assured, Ciano noted time and time again the despondency many Italians felt about the experience, their military weaknesses, the way the Germans were critical of their efforts, and those at the top knew their military supplies were low, making them dependent on Germany.

The Italian king was disturbed by the war, with Mussolini informing Ciano that all the king wanted was for Italy to 'pick up the broken dishes', with Ciano writing in his diary that 'I hope that they will not break them over our heads before that'.[19] Ciano visited the king who told Ciano that 'those who talk of a short and easy war are fools'.[20]

When Sicily had fallen and the mainland became a centre of bitter fighting it was the end of Mussolini. It is clear that Ciano, although not deeply involved, was part of the plot, and when Hitler had Mussolini rescued and returned him to Italy to rule a tiny area it was the decline of Ciano. He and Edda wanted to fly to Spain, but the plane flew them to Germany. It was widely known that Ciano had no love or trust in their German allies, and he was treated as a traitor on his return to Italy, was tried and following Italian tradition was shot with other traitors in the back.

There are a few published books about the life of Ciano, and when they depend on his diary, knowing the dangers of possible redactions they can be both enlightening and interesting.[21] Interesting because of Ciano's life as a fighter pilot, his philandering lifestyle; enlightening because they offer an inside perspective of Italy during this era, not just in terms of the war but the diplomatic wranglings as the Western Powers trying to steer Italy away from German influence. Because it is a daily diary, and despite possible redactions it is a serious form of Oral History.

VICTOR KLEMPERER

A SURVIVING GERMAN-JEW ACADEMIC

(**Writer's Note:** *Because these diaries come in three vast volumes the selected quotes are in italics and not end-noted*)

Introduction

This diary was written by a German-Jew between 1933 (the rise of Hitler) and his death in 1959 (under Soviet rule). He was a respected academic, and he only survived the Nazi regime because his wife Eva was a so-called Aryan though they both suffered the most appalling repression under Nazi rule. The diary was kept secret and hidden by friends as it developed, because had it been discovered he would have been instantly executed. His views and opinions are expressed in depth and with considerable vitriol about Hitler and his leading henchmen. He also covered the war years and the need for survival from the anti-Semitic Nazis as well as the bombing raids. After the war he welcomed the communists in East Germany, but as the years unfolded, he labelled them as the Fourth Reich. He describes in telling detail not only the barbarity of the Nazi regime, but the better reaction of various non-Jewish German neighbours. It is a lengthy literary work in two volumes, covering in three English translated volumes some 1,466 pages.[22] This writer wrote a summary and commentary of less than 200 pages in 2023 which carries the main impulses of his work.[23]

Klemperer was born Jewish, became Christian like many others for social-safety reasons, but the Nazi persecution was racist, not religious, so for them it was no escape route, only his Aryan wife Eva provided some protection. His diaries are typical home diaries, ranging from problems of toothaches, illness, the welfare for their cats, their first car, buying a house, but inundated with his political observations and how people were influenced by the Nazi ideology. He pulled no punches, condemning the irrational and immoral behaviour of the government, offers the rumours circulating in wartime, and his reaction postwar working in the GDR, the German Democratic Republic, and his changing views on Soviet rule.

The diaries were not intended for publication, they were never revised or revamped in the light of later thoughts, changing times, or altered to avoid repetition or contradictions. He wrote down every detail as he was unsure of its significance in the future. The diaries were part of his toolbox as he kept in them notes on his proposed autobiography and his book on the language of the Third Reich.

For any reader of these diaries Klemperer is an enigmatic figure, and the reader's personal thoughts as to the behaviour of this diarist may raise a few eyebrows. He had a difficult relationship with his siblings, could be cantankerous, sometimes bad tempered, and often suspicious about other people. At times he can appear over-judgemental, cynical, and sometimes unpleasant, not least showing little sympathy for someone's death, and rejoicing that he was still alive. He took his first wife Eva for granted, and there is a distinct possibility she felt restrained in her life's ambitions by her husband's career. When she died, he was naturally filled with remorse, but within a year he married Hadwig who was nearly 50 years younger and a student, often he felt guilty about betraying Eva by marrying a young woman who could not have children by him. However, he redeemed himself by always being honest about his own failings and shrewd in his judgments on what was happening in the world.

In terms of oral history, we have a scared persecuted man sitting in his study writing this diary, concerned about the Gestapo knocking on his door which they did many times. To give a sense of the nature of his work a few of his written thoughts will be quoted *in italics*.

Klemperer's Diary Observations

As early as 1933 he wrote he could sense the terror and '*everyone cringing with fear*' but it was a mild prelude for the years to come. He watched the violence on the streets, heard the propaganda on the radio, saw the torchlight processions, and heard Hitler's speech from Königsberg, writing '*I understood only occasional words. But the tone! The unctuous bawling and truly bawling of a priest*'. He admitted he had been depressed by the 1918 defeat, but it '*did not depress me as greatly as the present state of affairs. It is shocking how day after day naked acts of violence, breaches of law, barbaric opinions appear quite undisguised as official decrees*'. He was acutely conscious that as a Jew he could not be an Aryan and therefore not German, and '*I must be grateful if I'm allowed to stay alive*'. The 'Heil Hitler' salute was announced, and Klemperer recalled that once, a mere nod of the head had been sufficient, now it was a matter of raising arms, introduced to '*avoid suspicion of an attitude hostile to the state!*' Disconcertingly he heard from the cleaning lady that her postman husband had witnessed a colleague sacked for not saluting. He was irritated by some Jews as they '*were beginning to submit inwardly and to regard the new ghetto situation atavistically as a legal condition which has to be accepted*'.

By mid-January 1934 he was concerned that the governance and constitution of his university were changing for political reasons, with Klemperer noting '*no one dares to resist openly; each one is always an isolated individual, who feels powerless*', but all the time hoping the government would collapse. He wrote about Goebbels and his propaganda that the man was '*no psychologist*', that he was '*simply boring*' and '*binds the whole person*' and '*tyrannises him*'. It was fortunate, given the number of people who knew Klemperer kept a diary, and heard his cynical comments, that the authorities never discovered his writing. When he heard Göring in a speech in Berlin City Hall state '*All of us, from the simple SA man right up to the prime minister, are of Adolf Hitler and through Adolf Hitler. He is Germany*', which Klemperer saw as '*the language of the Gospels*' which was a pertinent comment.

In April 1935 he was dismissed from his post in the university, and in June he was depressed by the Anglo-German Naval Agreement, realising that the regime marked this as a foreign policy success. His feelings erupted on reading the Nuremberg Race Laws, prohibiting sexual relationships between Jews and Aryans, banning Jewish flags, and all based on '*German blood and honour*' writing '*the disgust makes one ill*'.

A year later in April 1936 he heard of the decree that civil servants were prohibited from consorting with Jews, and he was concerned they had not heard from their friends the Köhlers. This was the start of depression, in May writing '*I do not believe that I shall live to the end of the Third Reich, and I let myself drift along fatalistically without especial despair and cannot give up hope*'. Life for Klemperer was mundane, and as the events of history unfolded, he described his life as '*proletarianised*' as he washed dishes, polished knives, and found succour by retaining his '*freedom of thought*'. It would not be long before he was involved in forced local labour, from clearing snow to working in factories. He was cynical about the Olympics, raising a justified criticism about the '*over-estimation of sport. The honour of a nation depends on whether a fellow citizen can jump four inches higher than the rest*'.

In mid-August 1937 he saw the *Der Stürmer* paper for sale with two girls in swimming costumes but above the stand the notice '*Prohibited for Jews*'. This unpleasant blunt notice sent him into another moment of reflection recalling that for most of his life he had never been aware of anti-Semitism.

It was even more galling for him in **1938** when Klemperer was obliged to change his forename to *Victor-Israel*. He could not enter the library, borrow books, heard of the horrors of *Kristallnacht*, and two policemen searched his house for weapons. Jewish driving licences were withdrawn, and curfews on Jews were amounting. At the beginning of March Hitler presented Göring with his marshal's baton with Klemperer noting that '*they have no sense of the comic impression they make*'. The queues outside the American consulate were long and Klemperer was picking up '*fragmentary rumours*' about Buchenwald surrounded by secrecy but noting that '*no one comes back from a second time there*'.

At the start of 1939 New Year's Day he heard of the devastating news about the vicious treatment of Jews in Ulm where a rabbi '*was chased (by the mob, that is, by the people, and not just by SA carrying out orders!) round the market fountain with his beard alight and was hit on the hands when he tried to touch his beard*. Klemperer was understandably concerned that this was a public reaction and not just Nazi thugs (SA) under orders. This policy seemed to be taking hold of the public mind. He was always curious about public reaction and their thinking processes. He found it impossible to judge what he called the *vox populi* feelings, writing *'who can judge the mood of 80 million people, with the press bound and everyone afraid of opening their mouth?'* It was a repressed society and Klemperer recognised this fact. In the Jews' House Klemperer noted that everyone was trying *'to fathom the mood of the people'*, and all are dependent on the last remark they had picked up whether from the barber or butcher.

The war years 1939-1945 would make his and Eva's life more unpleasant and tenuous. Their rooms were searched, they were made to move from their home into various Jewish quarters, known as the Jew-Houses, and forced labour was the order of the day. As the months unfolded, he soon discovered that his usual shopkeepers varied as some became frightened to serve him with the anti-Jewish restrictions, with a few cautious but amenable, while others took the risk serving him below the counter indicating their sympathy. When he asked shopkeeper Vogel for half a loaf without coupons the shopkeeper *'whispered: for God's sake never ask the girl* [Assistant] *for that…and then in a loud voice "so the coupons first". Takes my cards and the scissors, cuts the air, gives them back to me and fetches the bread'*. Not all were anti-Semitic but had to keep their feelings quiet. More disconcerting was the rumour of the *'Lublin business'* with the deportation of Jews which Klemperer thought would make a *'terrible impression abroad'*, which it would, but only postwar. Throughout the war years Klemperer only heard the gossip and propaganda, when a neighbour Frau Voss returned from the dentist who had claimed England would be destroyed in a few weeks, revealing how the moods could swing like a pendulum dependent on the latest rumour or information, with Klemperer reflecting on *'what is the mind of the populace? The insoluble riddle'*, but thanks to his diary the muddled information and the hopes and fears are readable today.

During the war years because he was a Jew his pet cat had to be put down, he could not subscribe for papers, travel, buy electrical goods, ice-cream, stand in queues, the Jewish Star had to be seen, and talks of massacres were being heard. He was once arrested by the Gestapo on a tram when one of them, *'a young man turned towards me, very clean-cut face, cold grey eyes, and says quietly: "Get off at next stop".'* He had become of interest to the young Gestapo officer referring to him as *'my dog catcher'*. The interrogation was unpleasant, but his marriage to Eva stopped him disappearing. Klemperer noted that he had transformed from a respected university professor to a hunted animal, humiliated and spat at, feeling with good reason that his life was precarious.

However, on one occasion he was using a pram to push potatoes home when it tipped over, and *'a lady, turning grey with a boy'* rushed over to help with Klemperer observing *'she must have seen my star, it was a demonstration'* of support. In the workplace he talked with those he worked alongside, hearing about experiences in Dachau concentration camp, with Klemperer writing *'at least I am consistently treated with friendliness and a little respect'*.

By 1944 for the more astute the war was changing. There were debates among the workers as to the number of enemy planes, with Goebbels giving a speech that those *'bombed out, must fight on and win if they want to get compensation'* and the bombing showed the *'English cruelty'* with Klemperer adding what *'about the attacks on London'*. One of the residents in the Jewish quarters heard in a queue a woman state that *'the Jews really had been treated too badly; they were human beings too and all the attacks on Berlin and the destruction of Leipzig were retribution'*. This belief that the bombing was retribution for the Jews would increase in the following months as known from many sources. When he heard of the failed 20 July plot to kill Hitler Klemperer explained to himself this was useful for the dictator because *'HE wanted to give himself the aura of holy invulnerability'*. It was at this stage that he heard rumours that Jews were being gassed in their thousands.

The horrendous bombing of Dresden gave Klemperer and Eva the opportunity to escape with long dangerous journeys doing their best to keep their heads down, just mere German refugees. As the war was now seen as lost, the atmosphere changed, while Klemperer and Eva were eating with a policeman who was doing a check but was extraordinarily polite, even shaking Klemperer's hand, telling him *'things are going to change'*. This incident reflected the increasing change that as the war was being lost, many were wondering about the consequences of their barbaric treatment of Jewish people. Eva noted that many shopkeepers appeared to be suddenly helpful.

During the postwar era of 1945-1958 Klemperer lived in East Germany seeing the Soviets as their saviours and accepting their rule as better than the Nazis which was an understandable reaction. In return for his twelve years of persecution he now became highly ambitious in his new freedom, both in terms of his academic status and political involvement. The Soviets utilised his support and trusted him, and he was allowed into West Germany on official business. Initially he was nonplussed by Soviet inefficiency and the appalling lack of food as Russia stripped the area for war reparations, but more importantly for the diarist he was reappointed Professor Klemperer, and the Soviets had agreed that as a scholar he would receive a heavy worker's ration card. Sometimes with Eva, he travelled around the various educational institutions sometimes taking on new posts; he was pleased because he had become a 'somebody' again. As the years passed, he became wealthy by the standards of the day and respected. He and Eva enjoyed holidays including maritime cruises.

Such were the nightmares of the past he remained suspicious of West Germany often referring to them using ex-Nazis to help, and feeling they lacked political integrity. In his diary he wrote *'I am increasingly strengthened in my own contempt for mankind and my lack of vanity. I was treated as lower than a dog, now I am courted by every means – what will tomorrow bring?*' However, at times he had doubts about the developing situation. At a traditional Russian celebration, he observed the gigantic picture of Stalin bedecked with medals and '*the constant parades*' adding '*that's how antimilitarism is demonstrated to the Germans*' indicating that he had lost none of his cynicism (or realism). When he saw Stalin's poster again in October it reminded him of Hermann Göring. However, he remained supportive of the current situation, writing '*I no longer believe in the united German patria. I believe, we could very well cultivate German culture as a Soviet state under Russian leadership*', which once he would have totally rejected, and much later would question. His attitude was helped as the Soviets helped grow his sense of importance. This was understandable given that in 1933 he was considered important but for the next twelve years was treated as unwanted scum.

Sadly, in November 1946 Eva discovered she had cancer, needing a serious operation in 1947. He was often away from Eva on his ambitious tours, and he felt guilty when home. On one occasion, Eva woke him in the night telling him she had been chased out of her home by the Gestapo, and now with the journey to Greifswald it was happening again. This caused Klemperer to ponder that '*it was very painful for me. Have I sacrificed her contentment to my vanity*' which was a reasonable self-reflection. Like many old people he was critical of new modern developments. He had noted on a train journey that all the women were smoking '*all without men, on their own feet, morally quite free, with their trousers, their cigarettes, their children*'. He did not reflect on the likely tragedies of their past, but was more curious about women wearing trousers, stating '*morally free*' seeming to question their morality. Later in July while near the beach he noticed that the '*women wear pants and breast bib, naked in between*' further adding the '*big Sunday crowd, as if there had been no annihilation of millions*'. He seemed somewhat judgemental in these modern developments, possibly 'an old age' problem. Also, when he travelled back to Dresden he saw the new Democratic Republic flag, not liking the colours of black, red, and gold which reminded him of the Greater Germany or the Weimar Republic.

On 8 May 1951 Klemperer asked permission to absent himself from the Liberation Day, but he was told *'when the Nazis organised an act of state, everyone came, everyone had to come. We must manage that too'*, adding *'He was not wrong, so I stayed'*, but the Nazi comparison tested his nerves. More testing for him was the death of his wife Eva in July. Although constantly feeling guilty about Eva, at the age of 70 Klemperer met in 1952 a 25-year-old student called Hadwig whom he eventually married. He felt equally guilty being married to a youngster, but it transpired to be a happy relationship. It was the young Hadwig who help draw his attention to the non-democratic state of the Soviet control, and he soon became dis-enamoured with the system, referring to it as the Fourth Reich. It was a trip to China which put him off communism as a viable system of good government, becoming more aware of the barbaric behaviour of the system as exercised both in China and Russia. Klemperer was disgruntled about the politics of the day and in August 1955 he wrote *'very detached and disgusted with respect to politics – above all bored by it. Both sides lie, hush up, slander, I can no longer feel any enthusiasm for "us". I merely find the Federal Republic "even worse"'*. Politics had made him a sad and depressed man as only politics and humankind's behaviour can.

From 1958 Klemperer's health deteriorated; he died in early 1960 and was buried alongside Eva his first wife whose so-called Aryan pedigree had save him.

Final Comments

He maintained a diary which amounts to a record of Oral History. It was kept under the most dangerous circumstances, which if discovered during the Nazi Gestapo searches would have meant death, or through the Communist era imprisonment. This diary is important because it offered many unique insights into German life from the rise of Hitler in 1933, through the Jewish persecution, the Second World War and on to 1959 under Soviet and Communist domination. His diary illustrated the cruelty of the Nazi anti-Semitism while revealing that although many Germans were caught up in this evil, he offered the insight that there were others who bravely did their best to help Klemperer and Jewish people at their own personal risk. His comments on individuals, the information of their opinions, the *vox populi*, offers an insight into the German public at street level. Their reactions during the turbulent war years with the lack of information and their survival instincts, hopes, and fears, are instructive, and tell us much about human nature.

After 1945 when living in East Germany under the Communist regime Klemperer appeared to change dramatically. He became hyper-ambitious and as a one-time democratic person who had been both anti-Nazi and anti-Communist, he suddenly became a member of the Communist Party and distrustful of the Western Powers. It was undoubtedly a rebound from the Nazi era because the Soviets had killed off Nazism and for Klemperer the Western powers were not so efficient after 1945. The Cold War period and the East German 1953 revolt almost seemed to elude him with his new views, but eventually Hadwig's views and those of others, along with his own observations of what was happening in the GDR started to have a personal impact, and it slowly dawned on him that the Soviet form of communism was also tyrannical. It took time, but he was, like us, all too human.

Historians have often drawn the picture of this period with its political ramifications, military accounts, there have been some social histories of the time, but Klemperer's diaries provide a unique insight into the German public mind and his own account as a German-Jew who not only survived Nazi Germany but commented on it every day, as he continued to do after 1945 under Soviet Communism.

This amounts to an outstanding major work based Oral History.

JOSEPH GOEBBELS

MANIPULATOR OF MINDS

His origins

The now infamous figure of Joseph Goebbels, not just the Nazi propaganda minister but one of Hitler's main henchmen, will always be of interest as a man who rose to political power and was regarded as ruthless. He was intelligent and educated, but hardly the much-praised Nazi image of the blue-eyed fair-haired image of powerful masculinity. At the age of about four it was discovered that he had infantile paralysis, and following an operation this medical intrusion damaged his foot leaving him clubfooted. The biographer Reimann pointed out that the clubfoot was often explained as an accident or illness because a man actually 'born with a clubfoot would not have been acceptable to the NSDAP.[24] There were times when Goebbels would pretend it was a result of First World War injuries, in which he never fought. There has been considerable debate over how far this deformity formed his personality, with some writers such as the biographer Heiber, giving it considerable space. He may have been right, because with Göbbels' frail body-build and ugly features 'its emotional consequences can only have been negative. It is easy to imagine what the young boy had to endure, such as pitying glances from adults, no easier to bear because they were kindly, and ridicule from his peers'.[25] He may have developed intellectually to compensate for his crippled body, but many people have suffered these problems and did not become fanatically vicious.

Curiously, given his later well-known attitudes towards the Church, he appeared to take his Roman Catholic faith seriously and his parents, especially his father, projected that one day he might become a priest. As a young man hindered by his club foot, he may have perceived this as a way of gaining some standing in the world, as position was important to him even at this age. He had joined the Catholic Student's Association, *Unitas* which helped him with grants, while he pursued his university studies. Another strange twist was that when Goebbels transferred to the University of Heidelberg he worked under the guidance of the famous and much-admired Jewish Professor of Literature, a Friedrich Gundolf who guided him to work under a Professor Max von Waldenburg.*

From his youth he had a desire for women, and this was the start of a life-long habit, of a sex-addict. This addiction can arise not just from pleasure but from the sense of adventure, risk and power. At school his first girlfriend was Lene Krage and, true to his sex-addiction, he was to have many girlfriends, and later in life mistresses and lovers. It would appear during the early part of his life that Göbbels had little or no anti-Semitism, but he was disturbed that his new girlfriend Else was the daughter of a Jewish mother. The Göbbels' family lawyer and his favourite professor had both been Jewish. During the years of 1923-24 Göbbels started to attend political rallies, and it is clear that Göbbels was heading towards the political fray which would dominate the rest of his life. This was probably when his anti-Church and anti-Semitism took root. In early 1923 Göbbels was beginning to join the general throng of blaming the Jews for the defeat in 1918. Nevertheless, the first signs of vicious anti-Semitism in Göbbels can be found in his personal failure to publish his literary works which he blamed on the Jewish publishing houses. It was his failure to be seen as an emerging literary star which made him somewhat depressed at this time.

This was the early life of a man who was deeply ambitious possibly stirred by his physical disability to ascend the ladder of importance. His attachment to Hitler was evident from his diary which, when read, reveals much about himself, other figures of importance, including Hitler, and the diary also reflects his sense of self-importance telling the modern-day reader much about this era. It is possible to read Albert Speer's work, but it is known that it carries that sense of self-justification, whereas this diary gives a closer microscopic detail, and because he and

---

* Friedrich Gundolf was a famous national scholar whose original Jewish name had been Gundelfinger.

his wife killed themselves after first killing their children, there was no point in changing the original text. What must never be forgotten is that it was Goebbels who through his dominant management of the media and press producing Nazi propaganda who managed to propel many German people in the wrong direction.

Diary Pickings from 1939

On 13 October 1939 he wrote of the British Prime Minister's speech with its 'hints of conciliation', writing 'this old loudmouth produces a lot of words, but you don't get wise from listening. A Parliamentary windbag! How far superior we are'.[26] His attacks on men like Chamberlain and especially Churchill were always vociferous, and in his propaganda, he was constantly denigrating the leaders of other countries and invariably reminding the German population of their natural superiority. He was overjoyed when on 16 October he heard Lloyd George 'has written another article in the Hearst Press containing violent attacks on the British government'.[27] At the end of 1939 Goebbels attacked the Pope for his 'bitter, covert attacks against us', called King George VI 'sterile and idiotic, and accused the French premier Daladier of a 'hate-filled Speech'.[28] To have any form of compliment from Goebbels was unlikely unless he was referring to his demi-god Adolf Hitler.

The very next day he wrote 'another massive attack against Churchill with an emphasis on the *Ark Royal*'.[29] He had assumed that the *Ark Royal* had been sunk when in fact it had only been damaged, not that this mistake would have worried him. The following day he announced the sinking of the *Royal Oak* in Scapa Flow, which was a serious blow, adding that this is 'the kind of blow that the English cannot ignore' adding, joyfully, 'London can find no happiness'.[30]

During this month the liner *Athenia* was sunk by a U-boat which was a serious error, not least, apart from it being a passenger liner, it had many Americans on board. It was embarrassing for the Nazi regime, but Goebbels very typically tried to turn it to Germany's advantage, claiming 'Churchill had holes bored in her bottom'.[31] He was persuading himself and others with this evident piece of stupidly false misinformation that Churchill was trying to encourage America on side. He was equally as busy attacking Ciano the Italian foreign minister, whose diary is part of this chapter.

On 15 December 1939 Goebbels was back to naval matters, rejoicing that the *Graf Spee* 'seems to have given a magnificent account of itself. The three English cruisers seriously damaged'.[32] When the next day he discovered the naval battle was not what he hoped or anticipated, he wrote 'and so we tone things down in the press for a short while'.[33] A few days later he stated that he used reliable sources to claim the English used mustard gas in the battle with the *Graf Spee*. As with the *Athenia* and 'Churchill's bored holes in the bottom', Goebbels always mentions reliable sources when he is about to tell lies.

At the end of October, he was annoyed that the English radio had played some vulgar music for his birthday, allowing him to raise his vitriolic abuse on Jews claiming it had been done by Jews who had emigrated from Berlin. This was a subject he continuously turned to. On a visit to Poland in early November he and others drove through a ghetto, and he wrote 'we get out and inspected everything thoroughly. It is indescribable. These are no longer human beings, they are animals. For this reason, our task is no longer humanitarian but surgical. Steps must be taken here, and they must be radical ones, make no mistake'.[34] He never alluded to the fact that Nazi persecution of the Jews degraded the way they lived, and he and men like Julius Streicher persuaded some of the German public to see Jews as mere sub-humans. On 3 November 1939 he wrote 'the Jew is waste product. More a clinical than a social phenomenon. England's hirelings! We must bring this out much more in our propaganda'.[35] As early as November 1939 the use of the word 'clinical' indicated a dangerous thinking process.

He was blinded by the belief that the German race was superior, reaching a state of sheer hypocrisy when he mentioned Hungary as being 'brutal and selfish…she oppresses her racial minorities like no other nation. The Hungarian magnates are a real curse for their country'

George Patton with the four stars he prayed to God for. (*Public domain*)

The war on the Eastern Front where Josef Chervatin managed to survive writing letters home that all was well. (*Public domain*)

Field Marshal Rommel. (*Bundesarchiv, Bild 146-1985-013-07/CC-BY-SA 3.0*)

Rommel with his 1941 adjutant, Hans-Joachim Schraepler. (*Image taken from the cover of* At Rommel's Side, *edited by Hans-Albrecht Schraepler, published by Frontline Books (2009) and used with permission*)

Goebbels the pleasant young man, pictured in June 1934.

Goebbels the raging propagandist delivering a speech in August 1934 – his diary exposes him as fanatically ambitious. (*Bundesarchiv, Bild 102-17049/Georg Pahl/ CC-BY-SA 3.0*)

Heinrich Himmler with his wife Margarete and daughter Gudrun. (*Bundesarchiv, Bild 146-1969-056-55/ CC-BY-SA 3.0*)

The loving husband and father in uniform, 'the banality of evil'. (*Bundesarchiv, Bild 183-R99621 / CC-BY-SA 3.0*)

George Orwell, the well-known writer and journalist, whose views were always interesting and curious, had fought in the Spanish Civil War.

Statue of Field Marshal Alan Brooke, Chief of the Imperial General Staff, whose honest diaries caused a major stir when made public. (*David Holt via Wikimedia Commons/CC BY-SA 2.0*)

Ciano, Mussolini's son-in-law and Foreign Secretary, was executed by his wife's father. His diaries offer insights into Italy during the fascist era as Ciano started to turn against Nazism; he was aware of the plot for the downfall of Mussolini.

Victor Klemperer's massive diaries tell of his persecution as a Jew under the Nazi Regime. Many of his neighbouring Germans helped him and his diaries take us into their lives. (*Bundesarchiv, Bild 183-S90733/Kemlein, Eva/ CC-BY-SA 3.0*)

Marie 'Missie' Vassiltchikov, a white Russian émigré, intelligent and beautiful, who mixed at many social levels. Her diary tells us much about life in wartime Berlin.

Sir Alan 'Tommy' Lascelles, Private Secretary to the monarchy, kept a careful and perceptive diary offering some remarkable and interesting insights into life at the top of British society.

Ulrich von Hassell from the German upper class (Junkers) was a diplomat for Nazi Germany but turned against them and was hanged after the 20 July Plot. (*Public domain*)

Geoffrey Wellum (pictured right of the two), was a Spitfire pilot who, along with German fighter pilot Ulrich Steinhilper (right), wrote their accounts postwar, called reminiscent or reflective history. There is no reason to doubt their integrity and authenticity as they reflect on the war years, both filled with the horror of waiting for the call to fly into combat.

Amonsgt the realistic and edifying autobiographies are three frontline soldiers: Reginald Cambridge, Alex Bowlby and Victor Gregg, pictured here as a young man. It is more than apparent that they related their lives warts and all, indicating there is no need to doubt them.

(11 November 1939).[36] Across Europe, from Russia to Britain there were various degrees of anti-Semitism, but it was already known that German Jews were suffering appallingly under Nazi rule, not that Goebbels took this into consideration, because he was convinced and persuading others that they were more animal than human. By early December he was becoming more vociferous about Jewish people, and having shared his views the Führer, wrote that 'he shares my opinion on the Jewish and Polish question. We must liquidate the Jewish Danger, [Goebbels used the capital D].[37] The later policy of industrialised liquidation of Jewish families has many sources, but this early reference may put some of the early blame on Goebbels as he noted the Führer shared 'my opinions'.

In addition to the barbaric way Jews were treated, there was much internal criticism over the Nazi so-called euthanasia programme. This tended to shock more of the public than the anti-Semitism issue. Where the feelings of protest were, they were often muted out of fear, but some leading churchmen had the courage to raise the issue the way handicapped people were being killed for the sake of eugenics. On 29 November 1939 Goebbels, who was once supported by the church, and may have thought of being ordained, wrote 'the Churches are becoming insolent. I intend to make pastoral letters subject to censorship, too. This should put a stop to the clerics' abuse'.[38] It would not be long before many clergy found themselves in Dachau and other concentration camps. At the end of the year, following a discussion with the Führer, Goebbels wrote that 'The Führer is deeply religious, though completely anti-Christian. He views Christianity as a symptom of decay. Rightly so, it is a branch of the Jewish race'.[39]

Summary

It is seldom that foreign leaders are polite about political opponents during a war, they can stoop to ridicule and state as many criticisms as they can find. Goebbels is vitriolic in his abuse, at times sounding more like an angry schoolboy. He was an educated man but at times sinks into the gutter with his choice of vocabulary. He seemed fascinated by naval battles during 1939 and did not hesitate to tell lies, claiming Churchill sunk the *Athenia* and mustard gas was used against the *Graf Spee*. He used his propaganda skills against the persecuted Jews and hinted at their liquidation long before it started in the extermination camps. His attack on the Churches clearly indicated his youthful aspirations had evaporated in his new master Hitler whom he described as deeply religious, probably because he hoped the vague expression providence would support him.

This diary was virtually daily, and provides considerable insights into Goebbels, Hitler, and the Nazi regime, written as events unfolded.

MARIE (MISSIE) VASSILTCHIKOV
THE BERLIN DIARIES OF A RUSSIAN ÉMIGRÉE

Introduction

One unusual diary kept by an almost obsessive daily diary writer during the war years in Germany is basically a personal social piece of work, but with page after page throwing up insights of life in Germany, mainly in Berlin.[40] The writer of this diary was a Russian émigrée of aristocratic background whose family had sought shelter from the Bolsheviks in Berlin. She had been born in St. Petersburg in 1917 and died in London in August 1978. She was close to her sister Tatiana, and they moved to Berlin in 1940 to find work where life seemed normal, as the horrors of war and its brutalities were not yet apparent. Coming from her aristocratic and wealthy background they appeared well known by many of the upper echelons of high society of many nationalities. In her status as a refugee, she looked for office work and her typing skills and shorthand prompted her to keep a daily diary of her life.

When the diary came to light some parts were found to be missing, which could have been simply lost or deliberately destroyed. Some of it had been written in shorthand which Missie later typed out. The diary was deeply personal and not intended for publication, and some of the diary was still being worked on until a few weeks before her death. It is very much a personal account, but there are aspects which are of interest to anyone interested in history because it amounts to oral history (written daily) of events and the various people she met.

A useful guide has been provided in the published edition of *Berlin Diaries* in so far that an editor occasionally steps in with a historical version to explain what Missie was writing about.

Tasters from her Diary

Throughout her diary Missie constantly noted that she attended Church regularly, mainly Russian Orthodox. She enjoyed the music and singing but was obviously committed to her faith. Curiously in 7 May 1940 she wrote 'Have just got hold of a secret news item – Molotov has asked the German government to give no support to the Russian Church in Berlin', mainly because it was known that the only people who attended were Russian émigrés who were enemies of the communists.[41] Even as Nazi Germany was on the point of collapse and Missie was in danger all round, not least because she was a White Russian and the Soviet Army was pouring in, and despite the dangers on 1 April 1945 (Easter Day) she attended High Mass.[42]

People with Whom she Mixed

When working in the Foreign Office her chief was Adam von Trott who was later hanged by the Nazis for being involved in many plots against the regime including the 20 July Plot. Because of her Tsarist aristocratic background, as noted above, she mixed with many important people, not only within Germany but in various embassies. She was wined and dined in many expensive hotels and restaurants including the famous Adlon, on one occasion with some members of the Spanish Embassy.[43] Later she was invited to the Italian Ambassador's residence where the main guest was Galeazzo Ciano, Mussolini's Foreign Minister and son-in-law and well know philanderer.* This was widely known and Missie and Tatiana on saying goodbye found the Ambassador in a 'darkened room' where Ciano was 'dancing cheek-to-cheek with two of the flightiest ladies Berlin has to offer…we departed disgusted'.[44] This interesting observation about Ciano underlined her moral standards, and it is perhaps no surprise that as the diary unfolds it is evident she was anti-Hitler.

She even met and befriended met Gottfried Bismarck (grandson of the Iron Chancellor) who at first supported the Nazi regime, had held an honorary SS rank, but by 1941 was a convinced anti-Nazi, became involved on the 20 July Plot and managed to escape death probably because of his name.[45] She talked with Ulrich von Hassell the one-time German Ambassador in Rome who was also strongly anti-Nazi. She even saw as a friend the Military Commander of Berlin, General von Hase who gave her a *laissez-passer* (pass), which enabled her to take a bus journey even when they became restricted, and because everything was checked this gave her freedom of movement.[46] In mid-July 1944 she described arriving in a Berlin train station where there was disruption caused by the air raids, and she was helped with her luggage by 'the old Prinz August Wilhelm, the late Kaiser's fourth son'.[47] These are just a few of the interesting people she met.

Some of Her Observations

When she was in Berlin in January 1940 life seemed normal, but this was the time of the Phoney War, nevertheless she was upset by a government decree that 'no baths excepting Saturdays and Sundays'.[48] In Britain during the war years the public were asked to have no more than four inches of water in the bath. Later Missie was to discover this restriction on bathwater did not apply in government establishments.[49]

She found work with the DD which was the German equivalent of the BBC, and Tatiana at the Foreign Office (AA), but where she

---

* Ciano did not appreciate the Nazi regime, later turned against Mussolini and was executed.

knew her top boss was Goebbels. When German troops occupied Denmark and Norway, she noted that 'we worked like hell, since all these various *coups* must be justified in the eyes of the world at large'.[50] She conveyed a sense of distaste using the word *coup*, but it is curious with the benefit of postwar views that the Nazi regime considered the views 'of the world at large'. When referring to Chamberlain abandoning Norway she wrote 'many Germans have still a lurking admiration for the English'.[51] Like many Germans and Europeans she does not use the word British but English, this observation that they were admired by some Germans might come as a surprise to modern British readers today. It is evident from the diary that as a Russian émigrée she felt safe and comfortable in Berlin, but as the years passed by, she became conscious that she could not always feel 'at home'. She described on one occasion in July 1943 she and a friend were walking when she became aware they were being followed by a man. They tried to avoid him by entering a house, but he waited outside, and 'buttonholed' her when she emerged. It transpired that he objected to them speaking French together. She noted that 'this sort of thing used not to happen, but the bombings are making people more bitter'.[52]

Times were changing, and throughout the diary she relates the scenes of the bombing of Berlin. The fear induced by the siren warnings, the sudden loud explosions, houses and major buildings turned to rubble, the dust in the air meaning goggles and masks had to be worn. As early as May 1941 she wrote that 'now my heart begins to beat whenever the siren starts'.[53] Her descriptions are perceptive and portray the horror of carpet bombing.

On 9 June 1940 she related how the famous P. G. Wodehouse had been taken and persuaded to edit a newspaper for British PoWs and arrived in Berlin.[54] Wodehouse was British born but an American resident, and when he did a broadcast (which was harmless) it was resented so much he was banned from returning to Britain. In September 1943 she was shocked to hear that Rome had been bombed and later even more devastated when Monte Cassino was reduced to rubble.[55]

Her dismay was probably based on her religious convictions, but the Nazis found it excellent propaganda that the ancient monastery had been bombed to rubble, which was an ongoing embarrassment for the Allies, and she witnessed the number of photographs of the ruins the German press published with pleasure.[56]

On 6 June 1944 she noted the Allies had landed in Normandy, noting they had heard much about the Atlantic Wall which was 'supposedly impregnable' but now 'the long-waited' D-Day!'[57] She expressed concern about the number of deaths which would follow, but her exclamation mark indicated it was welcome news. This should be no surprise because her diary indicates she was always mixing with opponents of the regime, but how much she knew of their activities remains a mystery. This may explain why parts of her diary were missing, because anyone suspected of such activities was always in danger. She had noted in her diary in July 1944 that she had been involved in a group where 'we had been in discussion with a famous zoologist about the best way to get rid of Adolf'.[58]

In July during and after the 20 July Plot many pages of her diary are devoted to the attempted assassination of Hitler, today popularly known as the Stauffenberg Plot. Her first concern was whether it had succeeded, and the news drip feeding its way into the public domain brings this era very much to life. Her diary makes it crystal clear that it was a confusing time. She wrote of the day when she talked with Adam von Trott who was contemplating writing an article for the London *Times*, explaining why the plot had taken place. She warned him against this as 'the immediate reaction in Germany would be that they were in the enemy's pay'.[59] This she argued would upset the German public, which now the plot had failed would be less in their favour. It is known that to the very end of her life she avoided the subject as to how much she knew. She obviously liked Adam Trott and was worried for him, pleased to hear he was at home, then concerned to find he had not turned up in his office. The search for anyone involved or who were aware of the plot was long and detailed, leading to the deaths of most who were involved and even those who had heard 'hints', and many innocents found themselves in the Peoples' Court and were hanged, leaving their families in danger. It transpired, according to Missie's diary that in the future plans of the plotters, Adam had been forecast to be Under-Secretary of State for Foreign Affairs, which amounted to a death sentence.[60] There was constant news of even famous generals being rounded up, and she found it impossible to visit those on trial and took weeks to hear whether they had been hanged or sent to a concentration camp, which according to Missie was the same even with close families. She found it depressing and left her in a daze, writing 'wherever I turn, everybody is disappearing one by one'.[61]

By the end of 1944 she decided the time had come that she should leave Berlin. First to Königswart and by early January 1945 into Vienna. She and her sister Tatiana wanted to be nurses, which had always been their original intention, but their Lithuanian (their home) passports caused problems, though in the end Missie succeeded. Life was becoming tougher, no more Adlon Hotels but struggling to find food coupons and worried about Tatiana in Prague. Everyone knew by this time Nazi Germany had lost, and Missie witnessed the horrific bombing of Vienna, followed by serious problems with water supplies and lack of food. There were concerns that because Missie was a White Russian she would be of an unpleasant interest to the encroaching Red Soviet Army, but the diary makes it abundantly clear that she was a survivor. She was aware that she had widespread relatives and two of them were with the Allied forces trying to find their family.

Final Notes

On 28 January 1946 Missie married Peter Harnden in Austria who at the time was a captain on the staff of the US Military Government in Bavaria. Later they lived in Paris, and when he died in 1971, Missie moved to London.

Her Berlin diaries are basically a social dialogue of her life, but because of her background she met many of the minor key figures in

Berlin, and her observations, being diary notes, bring them alive. It is evident from her choice of friends that she moved in anti-Nazi circles and sympathised with them. As a White Russian she was a refugee living and working in a dangerous society, faced on the Eastern front with the Soviet Army who would see her as an enemy and bombed by the Western Allies. Her aristocratic background and wealth helped her in the early years, but it must have been her personality which made her a survivor by the end of the war. It is a form of Oral History because her diary was daily kept and brings alive not just herself, but German friends and acquaintances first in Berlin then Vienna. The *Berlin Diaries* brings this part of history alive.

OTTO MÜLLER-HILL

A GERMAN JUDGE

This diary written by Otto Müller-Hill, who was a German military judge during the Second World War, was first seen in French and not until this publication in 2013 did it appear in English.[62] The German to English translator wrote in the introductory notes 'so the past can speak as directly – not as elegantly – as possible … my translation is very much warts and all'. This offered some hope that this diary may reflect Oral History assuming the 'warts' represent the reality of the day and of the man himself.

It is basically a diary kept in the last years of the war when intelligent observers knew Nazi Germany was doomed. Müller-Hill explained it was a diary intended for his son and not to be published. At the time of writing, he was 59 years old, and his son was not even a teenager. It was very much a private diary. Nevertheless, there are questions any historian must ask. Was he trying to explain to his next personal generation that he was not 'bad', not a pro-Nazi, but always legally fair in his judgements, and/or was this meant to help himself postwar as he later noted in this diary that there would be recriminations. He knew this 'payback' would not just be international, but he knew German would also turn against German. However, the warts are there, and some readers will find some of his views more than distasteful, which conveys an honesty in his writing. He belonged to the upper echelons of Germany's middle society and was educated, and politically alert to the dangers of keeping a diary so he was grateful for finding what he described as a safe hiding place. He was right to do this because his diary carried strong negative views of the Nazi regime, and often criticising those who fought on for a lost cause. There are many ambiguities in his work, and some may feel it was the effort of a man looking to the future to find safety by being seen as a non-Nazi. This would become a postwar issue for many German citizens, which for any individual was often difficult to prove or disprove. He started his diary on 28 March 1944 and a year later to that day he wrote that 'they are a candid attempt to do justice to reality and to break free from the empty phrases of propaganda'.[63] This was the main thrust of his diary efforts.

Despite the various issues it is the diary of an involved man who used it to express his feelings at the time, and only the reader can judge whether he is offering an apologia, an excuse, or an honest explanation. For this writer on first reading the diary it was a mixed bag, something like the 'curate's egg', good in parts, or put another way, some parts seem genuine, others slightly overcooked. It remains a part of Oral History because it remains the meanderings of an intelligent German trying to evaluate the past for the encroaching future. As the diary unfolds it strikes the reader that with the writer's constant references and concerns about his wife Daisy and his young son Benno that perhaps his claim that he was writing for his boy holds some validity. They were bombed out of their house, and became virtual refugees, and the diary closes after the defeat and his final entry is about being stopped by French soldiers.

It is not the point of this exploration to unfold the book page by page, as interesting as it is, but under some headings give some examples of both his style and his thinking as the days unfolded.

Justifying his role

He was aware that during the First World War 48 soldiers had been sentenced to death but during the Nazi war it stood somewhere between 20,000 to 33,000, and he tried to portray himself as a moderate military judge attached as a non-fighting member of his battalion. He had to acknowledge that it was military lawyers who drew up the command for killing captured Russian Commissars. He was a man of experience as he had been a military judge in the First World War and called back from civil work for the next war. He noted that he wanted his son to understand his role, and also his views on his frank assessments as a military judge 'in what I am convinced is the final phase of the war'.[64] He knew as a member of the German military that 'perhaps I will be liquidated as an exponent of National Socialist tyranny who knows? No one will ask me whether I approved of all the terrible things or perhaps took part in them'.[65] This seems to imply he wanted his son to know as his diary would not be useful in military and political recrimination. He would have known as a legal person that it would be argued that the diary was started in 1944 as a preparation for the defeat ergo open to legal attack.

In April 1944 he was unhappy with the way French resistance fighters were being executed with someone called Fret saying, 'beheading was an option' to which the diarist 'objected in the strongest possible terms'.[66] Several times, with his reputation in mind for his son, he noted that 'in handing down sentences, I also try to be as lenient as I can'.[67] Later, near the end of his diary he wrote 'my mildness as a judge is probably the reason I wasn't promoted'.[68]

His wife and family are often mentioned in his meanderings, not least because of the danger they were in. He was aware they were 100 kilometres away and he could do nothing for them, especially

Benno who was only eight. He also knew he had to keep his diary secret because if discovered 'I'd be dismissed from my post and handed over as a civilian to the Gestapo for re-education. That's the equivalent of a death sentence'.[69]

The Inevitability of Defeat

He started his diary in March 1944 while stationed in Strasbourg realising that Germany would be defeated, although he accused many Germans of 'living in dreamland from which I fear they will be terribly awakened'.[70] Time and time again he 'rants' with anger at Goebbels' speeches and the way new weapons will hold back the enemy and lead to German victory, which too many believed. In May 1944 when there were rumours of an Allied invasion possibly in France, he noted in regard to Goebbels' encouragement and mention of wonder weapons that 'the people lap up such news like a morphine addict who's unable to live without a needle'.[71] In this comment he underlined the power of propaganda. He becomes furious when many of his colleagues and friends still believed that they could contain the attacks and win, writing that 'it's impossible to have a rational discussion with blockheads like him', 'him' being a captain.[72] He noted that even Count Stauffenberg and his fellow conspirators were blamed because they had by their attempt 'delayed the use of the new weapons'.

He noted that the newspapers were full of the battle for Monte Cassino and its remarkable defence to take people's attention from what was happening on their doorsteps. He realised that even if the Western Allies fought their way to the east, it would still be a matter of Germany being partitioned into small states.[73] He was not totally correct but was close to the mark, but then he also noted on the same day that he made this entry that the Russians were moving more quickly than the Western forces. Time and time again he referred to the logistical differences, with Germany's manpower diminishing, and the battle in the air being won by the west because of their obvious superiority. By September 1944 he was convinced the Germans would be driven out of France, and they would follow Hitler's order and fight to the last, but widespread panic would break out.[74]

Some found hope with the Battle of the Bulge, but the diarist equated it with the last effort in the First World War, knowing the war was lost. He was as angry when he heard someone saying that the British and Americans 'have been pushed into the Ocean and we can now turn our attention to the east'.[75] A curious feature of this diary is the way that men like Goebbels were still offering hope even in 1945, and according to this diarist many still believed him. He recorded on 27 January 1945 his Superior Staff Judge Kolb, who genial as he was, always believed the propaganda and lived in hope, but was now trapped by the encroaching Russians, leading the diarist to conclude 'that's how people are who live in imaginary worlds!'[76] Many were fighting for every metre of ground, and he questioned 'how long will it take to realise this?' Namely, 'we are doomed to failure by the stubborn hubris of the leadership'.[77] He was aware from his work administration that many soldiers were deserting, and he wrote that he would be curious to know the figures.

Draconian Measures

As a result of trying to stop the inevitable the Nazi regime was calling up young boys as young as 14 years of age, and elderly citizens, noting that 'the bleaker the situation…the more draconian its internal defensive mechanism becomes'.[78] He cynically noted that 'criminality is astonishingly low considering that everyone has been drafted'.[79] In August 1944 he saw a new order from Himmler that 'we no longer have Saturday afternoons and Sundays off', painting a picture of life in a dictatorial state.[80] In September 1944 he saw what he called 'small fry', some 14-year olds marching through Freiburg to help build fortifications in Alsace.[81] As a matter of curiosity he mentions the Werewolf operation which was a threat that following any occupation a liberation movement would strike back, conjecturing that either it was 'an act of criminal insanity by young activists' or came 'from

Dr Goebbels'.[82] He then mentioned seeing a gathering of 14-year olds whom he presumed were part of this retaliatory movement.

Americans

He appeared to have little time for the Americans claiming they did not like to advance until they had bombed everything ahead of their route first.[83] They wanted the enemy 'ground down' by the air force adding 'they don't possess the fighting qualities of German soldiers'.[84] He even thought that the enemy might find themselves with the problem of 'demoralised soldiers', adding he had 'more regard' for the British and Canadians, but later noting that the British failed at Arnhem.[85] When in October 1944 he heard that the Americans had failed to take Aachen, he put it down to the fact they did not want 'to get drawn into house-to-house fighting. They prefer to bomb and torpedo living space to rubble'.[86]

Warts and All

He may have felt sickened, or implied he did, on hearing about the Holocaust, but he was a racist like so many others in and out of Germany, writing 'in my opinion, we're already experiencing the decline of the West, when a drunken, uncivilised Negro can destroy revered sites of culture in seconds simply by stepping on a release mechanism'.[87] He appears to forget that drunkenness is an issue with whites and blacks and most races, and especially in wartime, and that Germany had bombed civilised areas of culture in many countries.

His Reflections

At one stage in April 1944, he sounded bitter at the Western Powers for not working alongside the Brüning government, referring to the Versailles Treaty without mentioning it (1931-32), pointing out that 'Hitler's movement could have lost a lot of momentum'.[88] Many historians have since made this point, being especially critical of the French policies. Later in his diary he 'thought that France was for us', even though he knew French resistance fighters existed.[89] He was probably basing this belief on some of the hopes Vichy France had encouraged. In his more reflective moments, he even attacked Hitler asking himself when will 'the least educated people see that Hitler's leadership was an example of not only immoral, but also possibly miserably poor politics, which mobilised the entire world against us'.[90]

He had been informed by 'Captain S' of the Holocaust, adding 'that is the truth, which unfortunately is not widely known in Germany'.[91] Later, in February 1945, he reflected that the murder of Jewish people amounted to hundreds of thousands of them, and later the reality of the figures of millions at the Nuremberg Trial would have stunned him. In March 1945 he knew this would be a postwar situation the German population would have to confront, writing 'is such a regime tolerable from a human and ethical standpoint?'[92]

Final Observations

As noted earlier this diary, started in March 1944, is probably an effort of self-justification or explanation by the diarist to his son Benno who would grow up in the postwar Germany. Whether it was an attempt to leave a good memory for his son or some form of explanation is likely, but much of what he noted was historically true and verifiable, and we have here a diary of an intelligent and educated German as and where he stood in the last 14 months of the war, a form of invaluable Oral History.

KING'S COUNSELLOR

AMONGST THE ELITE

Sir Alan Lascelles, known to his friends as Tommy, came from aristocratic stock, was highly educated, an intellectual, and fought in the First World War where he was wounded and won the MC. He was the Assistant Private Secretary to Edward, Prince of Wales (later

Edward VIII) from 1921 to 1929, resigning out of distaste at the prince's behaviour. From 1931 to 1935 he was the Private Secretary to the Governor General of Canada. In 1935 he was asked by King George V to be his Assistant Private Secretary, a role he continued for Edward VIII, then George VI, and in 1943 went up the final notch to Private Secretary, continuing under Elizabeth II until his retirement in 1953. Because of his family background and experience in high places he met many famous and critical people of special interest during the Second World War. He was a dedicated diarist and note keeper, and from a young person liked to keep a record of events. He never wrote a book, but his diary was kept and published, having been edited by Duff Hart-Davis.[93]

Naturally in his position with the Royal Family he records everything with care and consideration, but one of the features of his diary is his sense of humour. While travelling with the King and Queen through Canada in June 1937 he wrote 'The King, giggling in a most disarming fashion, knighted me in the train tonight, as the train approached Buffalo. I think I can fairly claim to be the first man dubbed in a train… so the episode has at any rate, some historic interest'.[94] He obviously had a sense of humour and enjoyed the tittle-tattle. He later related hearing from a senior Canadian officer that when one of Montgomery's staff has asked why 'he had issued a certain order' he replied, 'Because the Lord God Almighty told me to'. Monty, who had entered the room unseen, 'laid his hand on his shoulder and said, "that's right, my boy; that is how I like my officers to speak of me"'.[95] Montgomery's personality was well known and often ridiculed.

Later, in June 1943 the famous Stalingrad sword was being discussed, and the King had the sudden idea that the leopard heads at the end of the quillons [arms of the crossguard on either side of the blade] should be bears for Russia. Lascelles explain to the King that 'the bear was not, to the Russian, his national totem, but one invented by foreign cartoonists and to give him [Stalin] one with bears on it would be like giving one to the French ornamented with frogs'.[96] The King dropped the idea, and Lascelles noted 'Please God, he don't think of sturgeons in the watches of the night'. More than most significant diaries this one causes the reader to smile. The following month on 17 July 1943 the King's Private Secretary resigned and Lascelles took his place. His salary went up, he had a better office, and he would become sworn in as member of the Privy Council. He noted the time when there was discussion on how to make Turkey come into the war on the Allied side, Churchill told the Foreign Secretary to 'tell Turkey Christmas is coming'.[97]

In September 1940, he noted in his diary that a delayed action bomb fell at Buckingham Palace to the left of his office window and when it exploded it blew his windows out, including the windows of the Royal Family's sitting room.[98] Throughout the diary he comments on the bombing and later the flying bombs and rockets (V1s and V2s). As often noted, this made the Royal Family feel that they were in the same danger as the public which helped them relate to people when they visited bombed-out homes. Many of his comments are reflective and ring bells. When they were at Glamis Castle they came across some Polish troops, describing them as 'very warlike looking, with expressive faces which generally wear a broad grin…and most anxious to destroy Germans whenever and wherever they can get at them'.[99] It is well known historically that the escaped Poles as airmen and soldiers were dedicated and courageous to beat the Nazis, and they disliked the Russians as well with good reasons. Up to this point he had kept a few notes, but from June 1942 he returned to his need to keep a daily diary.

An interesting entry in June 1942 indicated the Foreign Office were already raising the problem of how to deal with war criminals, noting that 'they rightly wish to avoid a repetition of the foolish "Hang the Kaiser" campaign after the last war', but realistically, he added 'first you have to catch the hare'.[100] The more astute in 1942 were beginning to see the Nazi war machine faltering, but not enough to assume a total victory that soon, and postwar trials may just have been chatter over tea.

In July 1942 he attended a social lunch given for de Gaulle and his wife at the Savoy. For him it felt more like pre-war days, but he was uncertain about de Gaulle's value writing that 'we bought a pig in a poke there'.[101] He was already reflecting what was felt elsewhere, especially later, that the Americans and some British did not trust de Gaulle. Lascelles did not change his mind, writing in September after having been carting some potatoes, 'I was continually struck by the resemblance which the average large potato bears to General de Gaulle, though the potato is, of course, the more malleable of the two'.[102] In May 1943, Lascelles noted a telegram sent from Washington about de Gaulle 'as having no truck with him' but the British Cabinet refused to acquiesce – a rare instance of their not bowing to his will'.[103] Roosevelt could not stand de Gaulle as a person, but the British with many not liking him, including Lascelles stood firm. Nevertheless, Lascelles noted later in the year (20 June 1943) that 'our government and the American government are deeply dissatisfied with de Gaulle's conduct since he got to Algiers', where undoubtedly, he was tussling with the Vichy problem which Lascelles did not mention.

Lascelles was always careful what he put into writing, following the disastrous raid on Dieppe he refers to it as a 'commando raid' in which orders had been given to chain capture enemy. It had been Canadian commandos given this order, and in ignorance of the Geneva convention so the Germans decided to chain British PoWs. Lascelles admitted it 'was probably wrong' but tried in his own mind to placate the situation by noting that it was a temporary thing unlike chaining long-term PoWs.[104] In his diary he makes many interesting notes not only about the news of the war, but also events at home, referring to the disaster at Bethnal Green (March 1943) when in the rush for the underground shelter someone tripped and the crowd pushed on causing 178 deaths and many other injuries.[105] The pain of war can happen even in rushing for safety.

In April 1943 he picked up the news that the Germans had dug up graves of thousands of Poles killed by the Soviets, with Lascelles noting that 'whether true or not' it had made matters worse between the Russians and Poles.[106] This was a reference to the Katyń massacres, ignored at the Nuremberg Trials when it was suspected by many to be a Stalin war crime, but only admitted decades later by the Russians. The West needed Russia as an ally and the Russians needed Western resources, but Stalin was a difficult partner which Lascelles later noted. In August 1943 Stalin sent what Lascelles described as a 'rude telegram' to Churchill complaining he has not been informed about the Italian negotiations, but Stalin was demanding a three-party meeting 'but he won't go outside Russia' with Lascelles writing that 'I can't see how the President is to be got inside'.[107]

Occasionally, Lascelles comes up with some surprises. Halifax told him that Smuts had gathered that some of the 'smaller Allies (Norway, Holland, Belgium) would like to be formally admitted to the British Empire after the war'.[108] How far there was any truth in this rumour is somewhat doubtful, and Lascelles noted that since they had their own royal families 'it would be a sort of Holy Roman Empire with our King taking the place of Emperor'.

By May many were aware that a landing across the channel was being planned but it was being kept as secret as possible. Lascelles mentioned an American naval captain who had talked about the date and direction and had been sent home in disgrace, and an actor trained to pose as Montgomery to make the Germans think he was engaged elsewhere. More to the point Churchill and the King had talked, and both had agreed to witness the landings. This fact is generally well-known, but Lascelles' diary offers some interesting insights into this dilemma. Lascelles like many others knew this could be a serious mistake having the Prime Minister and King close to the front line, and even an impediment for those in command of the vessel. It has been claimed that the King agreed to discourage Churchill, but the King only stopped to re-think when Lascelles asked him about whether 'the project would be fair to the Queen and whether he was prepared to face the possibility of having to advise Princess Elizabeth on the choice of her first Prime Minister'.[109] It is clear that it was Lascelles who turned the King's mind, but the diary relates in interesting detail the argumentative fight put up by Churchill. Lascelles described Churchill as 'just like a naughty child when he starts planning a naughty escapade'.[110] The various subsequent arguments are outlined in the diary. Questions of constitution, such as the King having to grant permission for the PM to leave the country, and Churchill's counter argument that a naval vessel meant he was on British territory. It was pointed out to Churchill that if he were killed it would have a bad effect on the people and fighting men, and who would make the necessary decisions in the days ahead. It is a curious part of this diary, as it illustrates much of Churchill's stubborn character and the importance of the role Lascelles played.

When the news arrived of the occupation of Rome, Lascelles wrote 'this will sound all right; but strategically, and politically, the occupation of the Eternal City may prove more of a liability than an asset'.[111] This raises a few questions as to what Lascelles was thinking or knew and did not disclose. Had he reflected on the political damage done by the bombing of the ancient monastery of Monte Cassino, and that Rome was the spiritual centre for Roman Catholics, and should be regarded as holy, because on these grounds there could be political ramifications. He also mentioned the word 'strategically', and whether he knew that the American General Mark Clark had disobeyed Field Marshal Alexander's orders by taking Rome instead of trapping two German armies in the south was, if he knew this, too embarrassing in terms of Anglo-American relationships.

It was a world of secrets and debates and often contentious. Lascelles recalled the time when Churchill was constantly complaining of the slow progress in the Normandy invasion, writing that Churchill was 'maintaining in his rhetorical fashion that the progress of an army could only be delayed by the importation of dental chairs and units of the YMCA while Brooke' argued against him.[112] This debate had long been raging between Churchill and Brooke (His Imperial Chief of Staff), with Major General Sir John Kennedy writing about it after the war from his notes. Churchill was deploying a new description for his argument about unnecessary accessories, using the analogy of the Peacock which was mentioned above in Brooke's diary. Despite the general impression it was not always friction, there were good times, fun times, and as Kennedy noted 'the war would certainly have been much duller without him [Churchill]'.[113] This from many accounts was true and can be found in Lascelles' diary.

Observations

In November 1942 Lascelles had been very conscious over a great debate, accompanied with some anger, within the Royal family over a publication about the life of Queen Victoria based on Sir Henry Ponsonby's (Private Secretary to the Queen) notes. Lascelles wrote 'I feel strongly that nothing written by private secretaries should be published within a considerable time after their principals' deaths' but added the pertinent point that 'I don't see how history can arrive at the truth if contemporaries are not allowed to write it'.[114] The essence of Oral History.

Today's reader is fortunate that the highly astute Lascelles held this attitude as he gives many insights, not just into the Royal family who were essential morale boosters during the war, but what was happening elsewhere. He was very cautious in what he wrote, non-offensive, and all brought about by his background and the sensitivity of his post. He noted the issues over Stalin as an ally, the attitudes over de Gaulle, the Americans becoming 'self-centred', and many other issues, with the occasional comments on the war overseas and the effects in London. Above all, of all the diaries this writer has read over the last forty to fifty years, this one is given an uplift by Lascelles' sense of humour and the succinct way he writes, often causing the reader to smile.

JOHN COLVILLE

AT THE CENTRE OF 10 DOWNING STREET

John Colville, often known as Jock, started life in the British Foreign Office, then in early 1939 October he applied for a post as one of the Assistant Private Secretaries to the Prime Minister, and moved into 10 Downing Street. He was an assiduous diary writer noting that this new post 'would mean being in the know the whole time'.[115] He knew and admitted the keeping of a diary under these circumstances was potentially risky and against the rules, but like many other diarists persisted, possibly unknowingly, to the benefit of Oral History. In his time at Downing Street, he knew at both a personal and professional level not only Neville Chamberlain, Winston Churchill and Clement Attlee as Prime Ministers, but a vast range of leading figures ranging from the top politicians, diplomats, military leaders, and many of the government's top advisers, as well as many leading figures from overseas. More to the point he frequently expressed his view and opinions about them and the developing situations. One of his initial main tasks was dealing with the Ecclesiastical Patronage of the Crown which demanded plenty of letter writing, but more importantly he served three Prime Ministers during the war years.

He noted that Chamberlain, widely known for his appeasement policy, was 'tougher' than he is often portrayed, writing 'that nothing would ever induce him to deal with Hitler, whose supersession would be an essential prerequisite of any settlement'.[116] Colville had given Chamberlain's character some thought, and he wrote that the Prime Minister knew that Hitler was both brutal and untrustworthy, but he wondered if Chamberlain's vanity had been hurt by the Munich conference failure.[117]

From time-to-time Colville offers amusing moments, mainly emanating from Churchill. When, for example, a friend was worried about his daughter crossing the Atlantic, he asked Churchill if she would be safe, to which Churchill replied, 'Perfectly safe, but of course there is a risk of being torpedoed or mined!'[118] Later, when it was becoming evident that Italy was about to join with Nazi-Germany, Churchill is reported as saying 'people who go to Italy to look at ruins won't have to go as far as Naples and Pompeii in future'.[119] Later in November 1940 the same topic arose with bombing Rome with Churchill saying 'we must be careful not to bomb the Pope; he has a lot of influential friends!'[120]

One often overlooked asset of this diary are the many insights Colville offers of the hundreds of people whom Churchill met either at Downing Street or on his global travels. Colville in his astute and candid fashion comments on people ranging from Roosevelt to de Gaulle, the military tensions between Montgomery and Eisenhower, the issues of Hore-Belisha and General Ironside, men like Horace Wilson on whom Chamberlain appeared to rely, the American Ambassador Kennedy, the demanding Admiral Keyes, even Randolph Churchill, and the list is endless.

From time-to-time Colville comes up with information which sends the professional historian digging to find out further information. One such example was when two Englishmen had contacted 'high placed Germans…about the possibility of getting rid of Hitler and coming to terms with an anti-Nazi government under Göring'.[121] Colville noted the Foreign Office were more cynical about this than 10 Downing Street under Chamberlain. A curious conversation arose as early as July 1940 when the fear of a German invasion was high on the agenda, and Churchill instructed General Ismay to investigate the possibility of drenching the beaches with mustard gas, as he believed gas warfare would be justified under the circumstances, with Colville noting in his diary that it could be seen as dishonourable.[122] A month later there was discussion on shooting down enemy pilots, Dowding maintaining it should be done, with Colville noting that Churchill 'was in a very ruthless frame of mind'.[123]

It is his honest day-by-day diary in which he expressed opinions on external events which would later be proved totally wrong. The first example was his comment on a Government White Paper on German concentration camps which he said was 'an appeal to the lowest instincts' and claimed 'the evidence came from prejudiced sources'.[124] If he had wanted to change his diary postwar, he could have wiped out this entry as the eventual truth of concentration camps emerged as one of the greatest barbarities known to humankind. Some of his early views many readers will greet with mixed feelings. When referring to Chamberlain's gout, he thought some would want him to resign, but Colville queried as to who would replace him, as 'Halifax had not the forcefulness and Winston is too unstable'.[125] There were times when others such as Alan Brooke in his diary thought Churchill to be unstable, but time would tell because of Churchill's forcefulness and sheer determination to win, and he would turn out to be one of Britain's top leaders in all the island's many wars. In the early months Colville seemed to have little time for Churchill who was according to the diarist always pestering 'to be appointed Chairman of the Chiefs of Staff Committee'.[126] Colville probably felt this way because of his loyalty to Chamberlain, which Churchill claimed he was also and proved true to his word. Slowly but surely Colville started to realise Churchill's leadership qualities, and in April 1940 wrote that 'one of Hitler's cleverest moves has been to make Winston Public Enemy Number One, because this fact has helped him to be Public Hero Number One at home and in the USA'.[127] It was not just frantic working behind his Downing Street desk, because he recorded he was riding his horse at Richmond and it was the groom who told him the Germans had invaded the Netherlands and Belgium.

In November 1939 he referred to a discussion on bombing the industry of the Ruhr if Belgium were attacked. The general feeling was that it would be a mistake on the following grounds: it meant bombing civilians, would invite drastic retaliation, we would lose planes, and the French were too anxious about the plan.[128] As the war unfolded there was both tactical bombing of selected targets and strategic bombing (often called carpet-bombing) of cities and towns to break morale. Later the strategic bombing by the Western Allies was immense and met with criticism at the time and since.

Throughout his diary he kept his own personal commentary on the events at home in Britain as well as overseas in terms of the war. He opens January 1940 referring to an incident when a German plane crashed landed in Belgium with plans for the invasion of Belgium and the west. Like many others, Colville thought it was a 'put-up job'.[129] It may well have been based on the traditional view that the Germans were noted for their efficiency. This was known as the Mechelen incident or accident: a pilot and a friend were taking washing home, obliged to crash land, and they were carrying the genuine plans of the invasion. Hitler was beyond himself with rage and senior heads became less senior. When reading Oral History, it is critical to recall that the thinking or relating of events was of the moment and often dependent on rumour and personal evaluation at the time which could be way off the mark. It is, however, a reminder of what the thinking was at the time, whether right or wrong.

When Churchill came to power Colville described 'his anger was like lightning and sometimes terrifying to see, but it lasted a short time, he could be violently offensive to those who worked for him, and although he would never say sorry, he would equally never let the sun go down without in some way making amends or showing that he had not meant to be unkind'.[130] It is notable in the diary that Colville more often than not starts referring to Churchill as Winston. There are many amusing and bemusing entries in his diary about life with the Churchills. Mrs Churchill had been to St Martin-in-the-Fields and found the sermon to be too pacifist in its message, so she walked out and told Churchill who instructed both his wife and Colville to have the man pilloried.[131] Everyone, especially Churchill knew American help was essential, and Colville wrote of the time Churchill was sending a 'soothing letter' to President Roosevelt, and Colville wrote

'I was somewhat taken aback when he said to me, "Here's a telegram for those bloody Yankees, send it off tonight"'.[132]

As is well-known, Churchill wanted to set Europe alight where it was under Nazi rule and encouraged commando attacks on their coastal facilities. In Colville's diary it seems the idea first came to his head in June 1940, with the idea that Australians 'should be used for small forays on the coast of occupied countries such as Denmark, Holland and Belgium', an idea which grew rapidly, but not just using Australians.[133]

Colville at the beginning of 1941 decided he should personally join the fighting at first by joining the Guards, but while getting ready for bed Churchill told him he saw little point in granting him permission and would do so only if the need arose. Colville did not let the issue die, and a few months later in June started to think of the RAF, and by July he was pleased that Churchill had reconciled himself to the idea. Colville nowhere suggests this thought, but it is easy to gain the impression that Churchill needed not just his administration skills but his company, and this may have been true of Mrs Churchill who was always playing backgammon with Colville. On 1 August 1941 he passed his RAF medical and went into training, eventually becoming a pilot. He was called back to Downing Street on 15 December 1943 to hear that Churchill was seriously ill in Carthage and he was to escort Mrs Churchill there to be with him. He stayed with Churchill until he recovered and then rejoined his squadron in April 1944 for D-Day Normandy, but again for a short time before he was recalled to his desk. He was warned from time to time about flying, not so much because of the risk but because if he were captured, he would be a serious source of information for the enemy, but he decided against using a false name.[134]

He was soon back playing backgammon with Mrs Churchill and his diary turned more to world events. He was, like some others, sounding concerned about the American allies, noting that from 'the American papers one would scarcely suppose any British troops were fighting'.[135] There is no doubt that Britain was in desperate need of American help in terms of resources, money and manpower, but to this day this remains a historical issue. The British and Commonwealth manpower was strong, and it took the combination of America, Britain (and Commonwealth) and Russia to win the war, with each of these three components making the political claim 'they won the war'. The Russians call it the Great Patriotic War, the current American president Trump time and time again claims America was the victor, as do many British making the claim for their country. In reality it was because they were Allies the formidable Nazi enemy was beaten. Various arguments and statistics can be brought into the debate, and some cynics (or realists) might add the American support stopped Stalin advancing too far West. The gathering political tensions across the globe from Greece to America were noted by Colville as he watched Churchill's efforts 'to sooth the Americans'.[136]

Colville served Chamberlain, Churchill, Attlee, and returned again when Churchill returned to Downing Street. When he died in 1987 *The Times* obituary mentioned the diaries:

'The Colville Diaries – kept in breach of the Civil Service rules, causing Churchill to call him "one of the wise virgins" – are remarkable for their candour and for an almost Boswellian portrait of his master. "He domesticates the legendary", as Peregrine Worsthorne noted, "without trivialising it"'.[137]

It is a remarkable diary because of its candid exposure of the times, the major people involved and is of outstanding value to the student of Oral History.

ULRICH VON HASSELL

THE JUNKERS CLASS

Ulrich von Hassell was born in 1881 from Prussian nobble stock, he studied law and worked at the Foreign Office from 1908. He was wounded at the first battle of Marne, and he married von Tirpitz's daughter which embedded him further into the upper echelon families of Prussia, known as the Junkers, what would in Britain be termed 'the upper class'. He was a strong conservative by nature, proud of his country, and undoubtedly upset by the Treaty of Versailles. His work took him across Europe, he was Consul-General in Barcelona (1921-26), ambassador in Copenhagen (1926-30), Belgrade (1930-32) and finally Rome from 1932 to 1938. Here he annoyed Ciano whose diaries have been mentioned earlier, as von Hassell was not that happy with the Axis Alliance, so Ciano mentioned this to Ribbentrop, and von Hassell was recalled. Ciano was pleased to bid farewell to Hassell, in a 'cold hostile and rapid meeting', concluding that Hassell belonged to the Junker class and was not supporting the Nazis, who Ciano's master Mussolini needed.[138] There is no question that despite his dislike of Ciano, Hassell maintained a good relationship with Mussolini.

On his return von Hassell was placed on the reserve list of diplomats allowed to travel, and in 1939 was appointed to the main board of the Central European Economic Council. It was because of his work and travelling that he was able to meet many people from outside Germany.

Initially, like many other German conservative and right-wing people he supported Hitler's aims of restoring Germany as a major nation, which would have made sense to a person of his background, and so he joined the NSDAP, but for a variety of reasons exposed in his diary he turned against Hitler's leadership, not least because of the brutality of his policies, but probably because of the Nazi leader's derisive attitude towards the upper classes. It was this latter issue which brought him close to similar thinking men such as the Minister for Finance Joahnnes Popitz and the Minister of Economics Hjalmar Schacht, and Carl Goerdeler, who like Hassell, tended to want a return to the days of monarchy, and they became one of the conspiracy groups who were intent on removing Hitler from power. Von Hassell was simply appalled by *Kristallnacht* and equally shocked by the invasion of Czechoslovakia. He, like his close friends was beginning to be seriously anxious about the reputation Germany was accruing on the international scene. He was a traditionalist of the old monarchy school and was just as ill-disposed towards communism.

By 1941 on meeting Hans Oster and Ludwig Beck he heard about the appalling reprisals in the Soviet war and again felt it was destroying Germany's reputation. He and his cohorts and others who felt the same way became conspirators against the Nazi regime. There were various groups which did not always see eye-to-eye, but their common motives and intentions held them together. Following the failure of the 20 July Plot Himmler ordered the arrest of Hassell and many others. There is no satisfactory evidence that Hassell knew of the details of the Plot or even if an assassination was being planned, but he was a conspirator in so far that he despised the Nazi regime, and the photographs of him in the People's Court under Judge Roland Freisler indicated that he managed to retain his sense of dignity although he knew he would not avoid hanging.

His diary covers the year 1938 to the early part of 1944 and it is incredibly lengthy and in detail. He was a man accustomed to writing long reports, but even so he must have spent hours at his desk writing the diary. It first appeared in English as early as 1947 when it was published in the UK and USA. In Britain the publisher was Hamish & Hamilton. The edition this writer has used was by Frontline Books published in 2011.[139]

His reactions to Nazi barbarism soon came to light, as early as November 1938 following *Kristallnacht*, he referred to this pogrom as 'under the crushing emotions evoked by the vile persecution of the Jews…not since the World War we have lost so much credit in the world'.[140] He added later that 'the Bruckmanns and Karl Alexander were here for tea. Their horror at the shameless persecution of the Jew is as great as that of all respectable people'.[141] In June 1939 he was hearing some appalling information from the labour camps set up by the NSDAP, where he heard of a girl writing to her parents 'please do not beat me when I come home with a baby or I shall have to report you'. He added 'there is increasing evidence that things are beginning to creak in high places', not least because his traditional sense of morality was being challenged by these rumours.[142] He had little time for the Nazi leaders, on 7 August 1939 making the entry that 'Ribbentrop is behaving like a lunatic, unbearable in the office, and has lost whatever friends he had. Involved in a battle with Goebbels, is in Göring's bad books and of late has not been seeing eye to eye with Hess'.[143] Nowhere in his personal entries is there praise for any of the chief men.

In August 1939 Hassell called on the British Ambassador Henderson who was fatigued but hoped war would be avoided. Henderson told him about the British view, with Hassell writing it 'was similar to what I have written. Hitler must now demonstrate, he said, whether he wishes to be Genghis Khan or a real statesman'.[144] The English ambassador and this German diplomat had much in common, a sense of common morality and their social backgrounds.

For many men of the traditional German classes, it took time for the realities of Nazism to hit home. Hassell had soon been disgusted by the attacks on the Jews, had recognised the corruption within the Party, but often felt external factors were not helping. As early as July 1939 he wrote in his diary that 'everybody is in fear of war. The same old story between Russia and the Western Powers'.[145] Like many others in Germany and the Western World Hassell had a deep fear of communism spreading, but slowly he was beginning to see that Nazi influence was not only damaging Germany's reputation at an international level, but it was leading their country towards the abyss.

The reality of where the Nazis were leading his beloved country started to dawn on him with some of the information he gleaned from colleagues about the events in Poland. He heard that Polish farmworkers had been 'hanged because they had sex with German women', and when Himmler was approached on the subject he was told that Himmler was aware and replied, 'I have had the photographs sent to me, and have ascertained that from the racial point of view hanging was justified in every instance'.[146] Later, over the same subject

Bormann responded that the Führer 'takes the view that Poles are not Europeans but Asiatic and can be handled only as slaves'.[147]

Many turned against Hitler and the Nazi Regime as the war turned against Germany, many families losing their members on battlefields and bombing. Some Germans followed the tradition of never disobeying orders, others followed Goebbels' propaganda that all was well, but the vast majority knew the danger of opposition. The Gestapo and the SD along with informers were feared at every level of German life. As early as February 1942 this surfaced again in Hassell's diary when he noted that 'Oster and Dohnanyi visited me somewhat disconcerted by the news that the SD is watching them closely. The SD is also interested in Popitz and myself'.[148] Many studies and even films have been made about those who dared oppose the Nazi regime, including this diary written by the self-assured Hassell who felt concern at being exposed, revealing the nature of living in a totally repressed society. There were similar tensions for those living under the totalitarian rule of Stalin's version of communism, and to oppose the leadership of such systems takes immense courage. In its own particular way this diary which never raises the 'need for courage' underlines the strength of those Germans of the traditional style who were 'angry' at the way the Nazi regime was developing. They may have been right-wing conservatives, but they had not turned toxic, and many postwar years passed before they were recognised as a form of redemption in the face of Nazi degradation.

The diary is not a family diary, but more like a series of office notes written to record events which were deemed important to Hassell. He mentions many people whom the reader may need to check history books to identify. It is, however, a book not only full of information about the corridors of power in Nazi Germany, but of an 'upper crust' Junkers class German respected as a typical diplomat of his day and age. He stands out because although at first supporting Hitler, Hassell's sense of inbred morality was not lost in the hurly burly of war, but he had the courage to join the conspiracies against Hitler, even though he knew it was likely to lead to a death sentence.

Chapter Four

Recorded Notes

INTRODUCTION

Much potential Oral history can be found when reading notes retained as they were first written, and which can be found in many archives. They may explain the intentions and motives of the day, they may show that decisions were not always unanimous, and indicate political and military divides, which when measured by future events can be seen to have been justified or not. It is using a microscope to make clear the details of historical events.

The keeping of recorded notes also enables the researcher to see into the minds of people from the past, but they must always be measured and assessed. Many published books have been written on the Nuremberg trials, not just by the legal participants, but by medical experts in psychology and psychiatry. However, it must be remembered that under these conditions the real person under scrutiny may not emerge. First, they will naturally always be on the defensive, they may deny facts of the concentration camps, be critical of the Führer whom they once worshipped, and always trying to escape condemnation or preserve their reputation. A person under physical torture will say anything to survive, and although the Nuremberg Trial never deployed this method of interrogation, some were aware they might be hanged or humiliated by imprisonment. Secondly, because of previous thinking before the inevitable collapse of the Nazi regime, they had one argument in common, namely they were obeying 'orders', which was powerful because it was not just a Prussian military tradition, but this feature of military life was true across the globe.

As records of the time, these notes make excellent reading for anyone interested in history, but they would be more valuable if they were more like what has been described as 'armchair confessions'. This often occurs when two or more friends meet and talk openly and honestly about recent events and their involvement or knowledge and how they personally reacted. Confessions are intended to be secret, armchair confessions rely on trust, but if passed on some may be regarded as mere hearsay.

However, recorded conversations now published have opened an interesting door. In Trent Park mansion in north London senior German military officers, including many generals were carefully bugged in what they believed were private and confidential conversations. A Professor Neitzel examined the recordings and published these armchair discussions which throw a great deal of light on the various mindsets of those who led the fighting for the Nazi regime. This bugging system was meant to discover more about the military leaders, even including their strategy. Since their publication in 2007 it is like going into a time capsule, and hearing or reading about what these German military officers were feeling and thinking, and at times it is quite revealing. These recorded informal chats are like most casual conversations, having no structure, no hidden agenda as they were unaware that they were being overheard.

TAPED RECORDINGS

Of German PoWs

In this publication the recordings of the conversation have been written down and translated into English, and they offer many insights into the German military minds of the day.[1] During the immediate postwar years there was a general acceptance that the Wehrmacht conducted what was regarded as a 'clean war' and the SS carried out the dreadful atrocities. This attitude continued because of the Cold War and the need to rebuild the Western part of Germany. Field Marshal Albert Kesselring was sentenced to death for war crimes, it was commuted to life imprisonment, and he was released within a few years, because West Germany needed to rebuild the reputation of their forces. Kesselring was one of many, and it was not until the mid-1990s that an exhibition about the Crimes of the Wehrmacht exploded and became widely known. Nor was it surprising that in the many memoirs of German military leaders they painted a picture distancing themselves from the Nazi machine, excusing themselves by the tradition of fighting for their homeland, ignorance of the atrocities, and obeying orders.

However, these recorded conversations during the war years were an early exposure of the truth, making this publication an important oral source of history. However, it should be noted that many of these interned officers had been captured in North Africa with another group following Normandy D-Day. Nevertheless, the conversations reveal they had a wider knowledge if only through the usual social exchanges while they were still in post, with many of these imprisoned men obviously well aware of the atrocities in the East, and also of the concentration camps. From the earliest notes, they reveal the prisoners were like every human being divided on many political and military matters, some more than others. There were those who remained fully loyal to the Nazi regimes, some who were disgusted by it, and others confused and trying to adapt to their situation as prisoners of a globally despised regime. It was known and mentioned by some that some highly respected military men such as Beck had refused to cooperate, and others had expressed doubts while serving, and in Trent Park the prisoners felt freer to express their opinions with a growing awareness that they had allowed themselves to be misled. Their conversations were wide-ranging, from Himmler and the SS, the concentration camps, the nature of the oath they swore to Hitler, to whether Paulus had been right to surrender at Stalingrad, whether the Russians were still the universal enemy, and a rift over the 20 July Plot to assassinate Hitler, and often the traditional debate over military honour surfaced. This published record of the oral discussions among the German military elite reveals much of their thinking and the vast diversity of their honest opinions, and it is much more credible than later self-justifying memoirs, and in historical terms remains a treasure trove for understanding the mindset of these leading officers.

Eavesdropping, often by stoolpigeons, has always been used and continues to this day with police trying to uncover criminal activity, and it has grown in sophistication with cyber technology. Many prisoners would be well aware they were being bugged, but Trent Park was made both pleasant and respectful for the inmates, and it was established they were treated as gentlemen by gentlemen, the guards even saluting the German officers. The nature of their gossip from trivial moans about one another to major issues on which they disagreed clearly indicated they were oblivious to the bugging devices. General von Arnim had urged his comrades to be aware of the possibility, but it was disregarded, and von Arnim was often taped, while General Crüwell spoke openly to others about German strategy which proved interesting if not useful to his hidden listeners. Contained in the camp were 86 Wehrmacht officers including 63 generals, 11 Luftwaffe, some Kriegsmarine and one Waffen SS man. Of the generals most came from the upper class, a few from so-called noble birth, and 8 had seen service with the General Staff. By 1943 most of them knew the war was lost, later they feared they might face trial, some claimed their nation would fight to the last man and others questioned the sense of this idea. When the end-fighting was outside Hitler's bunker one group was seen to be right in their forecasts.

The inmates not only had their own groupings, as in any prison, but there were many differing points of view with some being highly contentious. The listeners to these private conflabs were not so much interested in complaints about cold coffee and English weather, but alert to any discussions on their political thinking, those pro and anti the Nazi regime, and taking careful note of the various camps of thinking and who was who, and where they stood. These groups would have changed from time to time with the influx of new prisoners, and the changing war news. Of some interest was the uniformity of criticism regarding Hitler's top men such as Keitel and Jodl, their weakness and subservience, which increased as the war appeared lost. Another area of interest was their particular thinking in terms of their politics and ideologies. There was always the possibility that within the camp were those who still adhered to the Nazi way of thinking, those who had become uncertain, and those who had opposed Nazi conduct from the start. In another prison camp the German General von Senger, who was deeply moral, and a convinced Christian was so trusted, he was allowed to wander on country walks outside his prison camp at Bridgend.[2] In Trent Park it was the divisions of thought and where the majority stood which was of so much interest to the Intelligence officers, especially the way they viewed the future, not least the Soviet Union which was of deep interest to the British.

The question of the atrocities was considered important, those ranging from massacres to the systematic destruction of whole families within the concentration camps. The men in Trent House camp captured by the British had been taken in North Africa and Western Europe, where war and life were very different from the East. Nevertheless, the bugging soon revealed that it was fairly common knowledge if only by what they had heard, and a few admitted that they had witnessed some such occasions. Naturally, even in private conversations, many wanted to avoid any such discussion. This would be true in any social gathering where the fun of adultery was under discussion, most would steer clear of such talk, many for personal reasons and some from natural embarrassment. In addition to this, as the possibility of war trials and recrimination was a distinct possibility, there was a need to be defensive through ignorance, and blame the SS. There were various debates over the killing of hostages when German soldiers had been killed, some arguing that this was internationally accepted, which it was not, but it had happened or been threatened by other nations in the war. The listeners also heard the views on other uncaptured generals still fighting, but mainly where they stood in their views on Hitler and the regime, which the British found curious about figures such as Rommel and von Rundstedt.

These recordings of private conversations have become an important element in historical research, not just from the point of view of German officers but humankind's reaction to ideologies and as and why there may be a change of mind. A leader who talks his or her way to power by promising a better economic way of life, more money, work, and power, may by a few be doubted for a variety of reasons, but when it does not work and war ensues, some hold a mistaken sense of loyalty and continue their support, while others oppose. In many German cases the sense of loyalty was based on Prussian military tradition with its belief in total obedience, for some they may know they backed the wrong horse and hang on because they are by nature stubborn and do not want to be seen as once being wrong. Those who have a change of mind is usually based on moral standards, and for a few wanting to change sides to save their skins. These recordings reflect the complexity of many dilemmas felt by many military, political, and ordinary people and although this study is about Nazi German officers it applies across the world to this day. These bugged conversations may not disclose new information about events, but they throw considerable light and insight into the minds, and sometimes changing minds, of those who were once the enemy.

Ten Extracts

Before reading these ten selected extracts some 16 German officer are mentioned, they are listed below in alphabetical order to see their ranks.

Bassenge, Generalmajor, Gerhard, 1897-1977.
Bruhn, Generalmajor, Johannes, 1898-1954.
Buhse, Oberst, Rudolf Gustav, 1905-1997.
Choltitz, General der Infanterie, Dietrich von, 1894-1966.
Crüwell, General Der Panzertruppe, Ludwig, 1892-1958.

Franz, Generalleutnant, Gotthart, 1888-1973.

Hennecke, Konteradmiral, Walter, 1898-1984.

Kreipe, Generalmajor, Heinrich, 1895-1976.

Krug, Generalmajor, Ludwig, 1894-1972.

Neuffer, Generalleutnant, Georg, 1895-1977.

Ramcke, General Der Fallschirmtruppen, Bernhard, 1889-1968.

Reiter, Generalmajor, Dr MED Karl, 1888-?

Ross, Obersleutnant, Josef, 1898-?

Sattler, Generalmajor, Robert,1891-1978.

Schlieben, Generalleutnant, Kurt Wilhelm, 1894-1964.

Thoma, General Der Panzertruppen, Wilhelm Ritter von, 1891-1948.

(1)

General Crüwell talking to Krause on the subject of Hess's flight to Britain.

Crüwell: I don't deny Hess's good faith in that respect [Krause having stated that Hess wanted peace with England to help the Russian war] but that is not my official point of view. No one but his superior officer, the Führer can decide about that. If the Führer repudiates him, I also repudiate him. That's that! I am convinced of his moral sincerity in that he wanted to do good, but that does not prevent my regarding him here, in an enemy country, in war time, as a traitor. There's no doubt in my mind about that.[3]

<u>Comment</u>: In this excerpt we hear a dedicated Nazi with a Prussian sense of loyalty and blind obedience following the leader, even though he accepts Hess's 'moral sincerity'. He also comes across as authoritative if not bossy and somewhat arrogant.

(2)

Thoma in discussion with Buhse on hearing of Italy's surrender which he had predicted.

Thoma: For this reason, I am regarded as a criminal by the others. I regret every bomb, every scrap of material and every human life that is being wasted in this senseless war. The only grain of truth that the war will bring us is the end of ten years of gangster rule. In my opinion the collapse of Germany is inevitable. I have been expecting it, and I only hope it will happen soon. I hope the end will come this autumn [Stated 12 September 1943].

Buhse: I hope the Russians will come to an understanding with us.

Thoma: That's impossible. It's too late now. it would have been possible last year, but our so-called leaders didn't want it. Every day the war continues is a crime, the men at the top must realise that. Keitel and Dönitz, for example are the men. They must put Adolf Hitler in a padded cell [associated with mad people]. A gang of rogues can't live for ever. It would be a pity if anyone of them was shot, though they should be given heavy work until they drop down dead. You will now see the English and Americans occupying the Italian airfield. They will occupy Sardinia and Corsica and then they will occupy France.[4]

Buhse: (rapidly changed the subject)

<u>Comment</u>: Here Thoma, highly regarded by the listeners, attacks both Hitler and the regime for their behaviour, recalling that as far as he knows this is a private conversation with another officer. This was a source of friction within the camp knowing that while some were condemnatory of the regimes, some critical, others remained loyal and supportive.

(3)

Here two critics of the regime Neuffer and Kreipe discuss not only dangers of dictatorship but mention the killing of Jews. Recorded 3 June 1944.

Neuffer: You can say what you like, but the highest generals did take part in that whole business, from 1941 onwards. There were certainly plenty of generals at the Führer's headquarters, who said: 'Certainly, my Führer', Jodl and Keitel for a start. You can't say that they did not share the responsibility from the way in which they let Fritsch be treated, in 1934, when Bredow was shot and Schleicher. Those were serious things. That was their last opportunity, in my opinion. Isn't that so?

Kreipe: Yes.

Neuffer: If you look at it historically, everything points of course to the fact that at any rate in a Western European state, which we, after all, are that form of dictatorship, which is pure terrorism, is impossible in the long run.

Kreipe: I consider too that all those ways which have been found of killing off the Jews are disgraceful.[5]

<u>Comment</u>: Apart from realising the dangers of a dictatorship too late, the phrase used by Kreipe, 'all those ways which have been found of killing off the Jews' infers he was not referring just to massacres but the concentration camps. They both regret the past, and now in the relative solitude of a prison camp realise the evil way their regime operated.

(4)

One of the ongoing debates amongst the prisoners was about how after the war the Western Allies would deal with Russian power. The overall feeling was fear the Russians would occupy and try to dominate Europe. For some it was unknowingly a prediction of the fears of the Cold War, for many prisoners there was a hope that the West would join with Germany to defeat the feared communist state. This was a popular discussion summarised by Hennecke in 3 July 1944.

Hennecke: The Allies are convinced they have won the war. Why are they so friendly towards us? Apparently, they shrink from the idea of letting the Bolshevists into Europe. It seems strange to me.

Sattler: I look on all that as a cunning Jewish trick.[6]

<u>Comment</u>: One man is nearly right about the widespread fear of communism throughout the Western world, not realising the Nazi regime was more feared, and confirmed by the ridiculous comment of his companion that somehow it can all be blamed on the Jews.

(5)

In this extract Hennecke appears again, this time his forecast is greeted by a typically more robust reply by one of Hitler's adherents…or was he?

Hennecke: It can't go on like this. Just imagine it, in three days there have been three thousand bombers over Munich and so on, just imagine the damage that is being done there and how it is increasing the chaos that will come later.

Krug: That's what I say too. What did the Führer say? And if they smash up the whole of Germany then we shall live underground.[7]

<u>Comment</u>: There is no evidence that Hitler said this, and Krug was probably referring to Hitler's existence in the Bunker and may have been sarcastic. The prisoners were not filmed during recording, and Krug may have had a cynical look on this face when he stated this view. Others agreed it was all futile to fight to the last man, they were military men and knew the end was in sight.

(6)

This extract is a conversation about Hitler between three officers.

Choltitz: I saw Hitler four weeks ago when he nabbed me for Paris.

Bassenge: What kind of impression does he make?

Choltitz: Well, it was just shortly after the assassination attempt, and he was still rather jaded.

Bassenge: Is he still injured?

Choltitz: He was more worn out than anything. He has put on 17Ibs!

Thoma: Mentally, he is ill, very ill.[8]

<u>Comment</u>: Choltitz had just arrived in the camp, and others were keen for home news. It was not a rosy picture of a jaded overweight Führer whom they talked about simply as Hitler, but summarised, typically by Thoma, saying that Hitler was mentally unbalanced.

(7)

Although many conversations in these recordings indicate many of the officers were either appalled at the mass killing of Jewish families, some were worried about having to stand trial for these atrocities, but there were some who continued to believe the Jews were by their existence a threat; a totally irrational view built in by Nazi ideology.

Schlieben: I can see quite clearly that all this Bolshevism is nothing but a colossal Jewish plot.

Ramcke: One day history will say the Führer was right in recognising this great Jewish danger threatening all nations and in realising the Jewish communist threat to Europe from the east…this is Jewish Bolshevism spreading over Europe and the Asiatic steppes, a tide we had to stem.[9]

<u>Comment</u>: he went on to argue that all the European countries were short-sighted to the nature of this threat and countries like Germany, France, and Belgium simply quarrelled amongst themselves, with England not helping with its petty interests in Czechoslovakia and the Danzig Corridor, proving the Führer right. This war created many immoral and often illegal moments of behaviour by all sides,

but the Holocaust stands out as a prime example of political evil, and ironically this conversation was recorded on 27 January 1945, when Auschwitz was liberated by the Soviet Communists and is now known as Holocaust Day worldwide.

(8)

There were others in the same prison who looked at such immoral and illegal crimes, two such men held the following taped conversation.

Ross: Before I was captured everyone realised that it would be madness to continue the war but none of the higher authorities had the courage to take a firm stand.

Bruhn: But they didn't know how many people have been shot and what has gone on in concentration camps. We have sinned, not you and I personally, but all of us as representatives of this system which has broken every moral code in the world.[10]

<u>Comment</u>: The camp recordings clearly indicate longstanding divisions of opinion, between those who still saw Jews as a threat, as subhumans, and those who knew this was not only wrong, but universally regarded as immoral.

(9)

In May 1945 when Germany was finally defeated, millions of Germans had been killed, criminal trials were to be held, and how much Germany would be governed by the Soviet Union was in the air, the reality must have struck home to those in Trent House prison. To those not expecting to stand trial, it must have felt almost comfortable and safe. Doubts were expressed not only about the future but the past, especially concerning the role of Hitler.

Franz: [Referring to news of Hitler's death] There has never been such a collapse of a nation.

Reiter: Frightful.

Franz: With so many resulting problems and concomitant symptoms.

Reiter: The Führer is by no means the greatest scoundrel, the greatest criminal.

Franz: I am sure he is not (the listener noted he said this emphatically). He is certainly not.

Reiter: He is a tragic figure, surrounded by incompetent, criminally disposed people.

Franz: They made him into one themselves in the end. Naturally he had a certain leaning that way. They would not have succeeded with any other, normal person.

Reiter: No.[11]

<u>Comment</u>: This reflects the dilemma many German officers found themselves in when they had to adapt to changed circumstances, not just the unthinkable defeat, but the incoming news of many criminal activities as the horrors of the concentration camps became public knowledge. Somehow, with a delicacy for one another's feelings it was a matter of gently removing Hitler from his perch. Times were rapidly changing, views and attitudes as well, but the camp inmates remained divided.

(10)

It was not just the annihilation of Jews which popped up in discussion, but the order to kill Russian Commissars when caught, the killing of partisans without trial as well as the shooting of hostages. In this extract the two speakers had frequently clashed in their views.

Thoma: The atrocities perpetrated by the SS and the shootings and the mass executions at Pskip (?) and at Minsk – two pages of typescript which I sent to the OKW. I received no reply. I established that no soldiers were ever involved, only a special detachment of the SS. They introduced the name of 'Rollkommando'. It's no good denying it. Of course, these people have become completely brutalised by months of such conduct.

Crüwell: I am the last one to want to defend such atrocities but, taking the broad view, you must admit that we were bound to take the most incredible severe measures to combat the illegal guerrilla warfare in those vast territories.

Thoma: Yes, but the women had nothing to do with it. Orders were actually given that all Jews were to be cleared out of the occupied territories – that is the great idea, but, of course, there are so many in the east that you don't know where to start.[12]

<u>Comment</u>: It is interesting to note that Thoma was disassociating the Wehrmacht from mass killings and atrocities by accusing the SS, which was a major factor in these criminal activities, but the Wehrmacht was often involved though only accepted as a pertinent fact as late as the 1990s. In this extract these two old opponents were still sparring with one another but with some care: Crüwell trying to persuade Thoma that some brutal action was militarily necessary, and Thoma half-agreeing but asking why this had to include women.

It was a strenuous time for the prisoners because some knew they could be standing trial, and others were concerned not only about their own reputations but that of Germany and Germans. Time and time again throughout the recordings are those who have heard of the gassing and massacres, a few admitted they had witnessed some such events, but there was an effort, even in private conversations, to steer away from such events. Also re-occurring many times is the mention of the SS involvement in criminal acts, which meant in their own minds the SS, although deservedly so, were already being used as scapegoat to keep a good image of the Wehrmacht. Another major discussion of having a mutual prepared defence in case of a trial which later emerged at Nuremberg as the tradition of obeying orders.

Final Comments

Only ten extracts have been quoted from some 167 documents, and they only give a taste of the various insights which were gleaned. Some of the taped conversations may well have lasted at least half-an-hour, others were much shorter. It would be looking at old photographs which have not been tampered with by AI and similar means, and it gives the opportunity of seeing and feeling the atmosphere of the day. As one looks at an old photograph, it is like standing in a time capsule, not just looking at the figures of various people and the telling looks on their faces, but what else is in the room which may be of significance.

The variety of taped people in these recordings is widespread, and some key figures stand out throughout the text. Thoma and Crüwell tend to represent the two extremes. Crüwell being a steadfast supporter of the regime to the bitter end, initially dedicated to its support, and even at the end still being defensive. Thoma, from the very start, expressed serious doubts about Hitler and 'his gangsters', and condemned the illegal orders and the atrocities. As with General von Senger mentioned in the text, Thoma's views and attitudes may have seen him used in the new West Germany, but sadly he died in 1948, probably from medical problems having had to have a leg amputated.

Between these two figures of Thoma and Crüwell were many groups, some supporting the extreme pro-Nazis and those who were deeply critical, and many growing uncertain as to where they stood. As the war unfolded many changed their minds to one degree or another. For some with Hitler dead, the oath no longer bound them, for others the imminence of defeat closed the matter, some were horrified on hearing of the Holocaust and other massacres, others wanted to be seen in a better light with the rumours of trials circulating. For as many inmates there were the same number of thoughts and mind-changes which reflect the human condition.

As noted above, it was abundantly clear that none of the prisoners realised they were being taped, and their honest answers were not changed or tinged as they would be in serious or mild form of interrogation. They were not talking with a suspected enemy or even a neutral, but chatting amongst their own type, their military colleagues. Listening to the bugged conversations or reading them is a passage back in time and this form of oral history is more than fascinating, allowing many insights into the minds of men who were once the dreaded and hated enemy.

THE NUREMBERG INTERVIEWS

Inside the Minds of Nazi Leaders

Reading the official reports of the Nuremberg Trial is a form of Oral History as they were a report of everything said on the lengthy occasion. The defendants were all fighting for their lives or hoping to avoid long prison sentences. When read, this must always be borne in mind as they would have been on the defensive, and often the truth was hidden by newly developed attitudes, ranging from ignorance of events to obeying orders and having no choice.

Of major interest is the work of Leon Goldensohn, an American psychiatrist who was there to monitor their mental health and stability. He was experienced and well-qualified and unquestionably, like many of his colleagues, wanted to know what 'made these prisoners tick', as some of them had been involved or knew about some crimes which appeared worse than the days of Genghis Khan. He wanted to study the pathology of their minds. He kept careful notes of many interviews and later typed them out, but with no intention of producing a book. Like the others in the medical team, for them the defendants were subjects of study. The defendants sometimes welcomed their almost friendly presence but once in court most would be trying to escape serious punishment, and Goldensohn was aware of this feature even in medical interviews. He made a point of being as neutral as possible and friendly, but he never held back from expressing his views, which occasionally meant being somewhat sceptical about some of their proposed defences. He had the impression that the Nazis were sadists, which may have been true of some but not all, but by now there was more detailed knowledge of the extermination camps, and it was all too easy to think this way. Only Rudolf Hess was mentally ill and possibly Hans Frank. Goldensohn left the army service in 1946 and kept his notes and typed out interviews which were retained by his widow when he died in 1961. In 1983 she gave them to her children and from that date they were processed for publication, a book of some 200,000 words.[13]

They make for interesting Oral History as there was no need for the notes taken at the time of writing to be changed. They are so lengthy and full of detail the best method for this book, which is about 'tasting' Oral History, seems to offer the name of the subject (as in the book under study they are in alphabetical order based on surnames) and to offer four defendants who caught this writer's eye as of interest for various reasons.

Karl Dönitz (1891-1980)

At the start of the *Second World War he was supreme commander (Konteradmiral [rear admiral]) of U-boat arm, from 1943 Grand Admiral to the German Fleet, and appointed Hitler's successor. Sentenced to ten years.*

Although Dönitz was a committed Nazi in the early stages, undoubtedly because of the Versailles Treaty, many felt his sentence was unjustified. However ruthless submarine warfare was, some argue that his crews acted better in moral terms than some allied commanders. Postwar many studies raised the *Laconia* issue, a liner sunk by mistake, with the involved U-boat risking everything to save them – and having Dönitz's backing. He had the total support of U-boat commanders who prepared from their prisons a statement that he had never issued an order to kill survivors. Goldenson wrote that 'the Chief of Staff of an American admiral, who was visiting the trials, had personally conveyed his greetings' and the American admiral said that he held him 'in the highest esteem'.[14]

Goldensohn was more interested in the Holocaust and asked if the navy had anti-Semitic policies. Donitz replied 'None at all. I had four Jewish high officers that I can think off at the moment. One was Rogge, a vice admiral who was in charge of the education of naval cadets…another was a captain. I had an affidavit from Rogge for my defence'.[15] It seemed plausible that he was telling the truth, not least with a submitted affidavit from a senior Jewish naval officer. This was not just a curious piece of evidence, but something of an eye-opener about Hitler's selected successor who ensued during his brief time as national leader and who kept Himmler at a distance.

Hermann Göring (1893-1946)

He was known as the Commander in Chief of the Luftwaffe, prime minister of Prussia, president of the Reichstag, and founded the Gestapo. He had been an early supporter of Hitler, was a well-known egotist, stole art from across Europe, loved dressing up and showing off. He was a bully and even at Nuremberg it was found necessary at times to separate him from other colleagues because he would influence or even terrify them. He was clever, and during the trial proved capable of clever argument, often to the frustration of the prosecution. Two hours before he was due to be hanged, he managed, somehow, to commit suicide in his cell.

Goldensohn described Göring as 'childlike', 'always playing to the public' and 'cheerfully usually, on other occasions definitely glum, chin in his hand'.[16] Goldensohn, as always, was interested in the Holocaust and did his best to fathom out Göring's involvement. He started casually asking Göring if the Jews had too much influence and Göring replied 'Yes, I guess so. In Berlin Jews controlled almost 100 per cent of the theatres and cinemas'.[17] Göring had always portrayed himself as the chief German patron of German art and its kindred activities. [He never mentioned that when he had been wounded in the Munich putsch it had been a Jewish couple who had offered him assistance.]

Göring was astute enough to know that the issue of liquidating the Jewish European population would lead to the hangman. He was safe as the head of the Luftwaffe, even after bombing, and because the allies had utilised strategic or carpet bombing to a greater extent, it was never raised by agreement. His defence was to polarise in two distinct areas, being ignorant of the Holocaust and obeying the Führer. He would tell Goldensohn that Hitler 'was a genius' and that he personally was closer to the people than Hitler who was always addressed as 'my Führer' but he was 'called Hermann'.[18]

In court when evidence was given by eyewitnesses from Auschwitz and films shown he either took his earphones off or looked away pretending he was horror struck. In terms of Hitler he tried to bully other defendants into agreement which was why the guards often made him eat alone. He explained to Goldensohn that 'we didn't know of innocent people being exterminated. I heard the name Eichmann here for the first time. That Jews should be evacuated from Germany was clear, that the Jews should go to the general government in Poland was also clear. But not that they should be exterminated'.[19] In terms of the anti-Semitism Göring told Goldensohn that he tended to blame it on Goebbels who used it to gain personal power.[20] It was a common ploy by many of the defendants to shift the blame onto Goebbels, Himmler, Bormann and anyone else who was dead or missing. In Göring's case he was happy to comment to Goldensohn on any of the other defendants.

When asked directly, Göring claimed he had never been anti-Semitic and would never have been interested in the Nazi movement if he had thought it part of their policy. Göring would blame everyone but himself. He suggested that in the final days Hitler was unbalanced because of the Russian shelling and the Allied bombers, and he claimed that Dönitz had been selected to be the last leader because Göring was too important and a symbol of Germany, while Dönitz was just a 'little admiral'.[21] Later he told Goldensohn that 'in the German state, I was the chief opponent of Communism. I admit freely and proudly that it was I who created the first concentration camps in order to put Communists in them'.[22] In saying this he knew the Western Powers were anxious about their communist allies. Finally he explained to Goldensohn that Germany would always need a strong leader, perhaps hinting that could be him.

It was clear that Göring was clever and could be charming as many found him, but his self-conceit about his importance was simply unbelievable, his ego knew no bounds, even in prison. He saw himself as second to Hitler but more popular, and there was a hint he would still be needed to lead Germany. He was despised and feared by the other defendants, he obviously lied about the knowledge of the Holocaust, he was cunning, but not enough to avoid a death sentence

Joachim von Ribbentrop (1893-1946)

He was the Foreign Minister for Nazi Germany from 1938 to 1945 and had been the German Ambassador to Britain. He was sentenced to hanging.

According to Goldensohn Ribbentrop had two dominating themes running through his mind, the first was whether Hitler knew of the atrocities, and the second was how the disaster of sitting in an international court of law could happen to him. In trying to encourage him to open up Goldensohn asked about the time he first went to the Court of St. James and gave the king a Hitler salute. Ribbentrop said the British press had 'taken it badly' but the 'king was very understanding, and the next day sent a note' that all was well.[23] It may not have occurred to him the king was the better diplomat. Very much like Göring, Ribbentrop suggested that in the final months Hitler was ill from the fatigue of the war on his doorstep, and even in April 1945 was still convinced the war could be won. This is perhaps suggestive that he had been one of those influenced by Göring, intimating he had a weak personality.

He even suggested to Goldensohn that Hitler's anti-Semitism was because President Roosevelt relied on too many Jews. Goldensohn wrote that Ribbentrop 'is quite an affected fellow, but his affectation is so practised it is almost natural'.[24] Goldensohn's views were perceptive given the views of many who knew Ribbentrop, and he described him as having 'the air at times of a ham actor taking the part of the great statesman who has become a little foggy because of all he has undergone'.[25] Ribbentrop tended to offer monologues (very much like Hitler) one of which Goldensohn heard was about Hitler's 'great personality. How charming, diplomatic, magnetic he was. how he could hold the whole of Germany in his palm'.[26] Ribbentrop offered a belated plea to Goldensohn that he had never realised how cruel Hitler could be, like many others hoisting the blame on the safely dead Hitler.

His opinions on what had happened seem on reading them today to have been almost farcical. He brushed aside the Holocaust saying it would only be a blot on German history, and told Goldensohn 'if only these American bankers had intervened and threatened England, forced her to accept Hitler's peace offers', hinting Hitler wanted peace and American financiers could have helped more by persuading the British.[27] He then went on to claim Hitler only wanted the Sudetenland, the Polish Corridor and trade agreement with Austria. For a so-called diplomat he was living in 'cloud cuckoo land' and being full of self-importance though his views were valuable. He also continued to argue that Hitler had a 'brutal side to him as well as a decent side…which appealed to me'.

He was upset that the British press kept 'referring to him as an ex-champagne salesman' but after reading his conversations with Goldensohn it is easy to arrive at the conclusion that for once the press writers were correct.

Julius Streicher (1885-1946)
Streicher was the founder and editor of 'Der Stürmer', the anti-Semitic journal. He was sentenced to hanging.

Streicher with his obsessive hatred of Jews stirred up considerable hatred of Jewish people, his paper *Der Stürmer* telling the most outrageous lies about them and full of cartoons mocking and berating them, all based on lies and the usual anti-Semitic myths. He told Goldensohn that 'I know more about the Jews than the Jews do themselves', telling Dr Gilbert, Goldensohn's colleague, that he was Jewish which he could tell by the way he spoke.[28] Goldensohn concluded on meeting him that he was probably of limited normal intelligence but generally ignorant, and was obsessed with anti-Semitism which 'served as an outlet for his sexual conflicts, as evidenced by his preoccupation with pornography'.[29] Streicher described circumcision as a 'Jewish plot' to preserve the purity of their stock, and accused Christ's mother of being a whore because no one believed the immaculate conception, smiling as he said so, and said he would not have that printed. Goldensohn decided he had the characteristics of an old psychopathic personality. When asked about the extermination of the Jews he simply replied, 'I had nothing to do with it' and would have preferred to have them transported to Madagascar.

He accused the American prosecutor Jackson of being Jewish and that his real name was Jacobson. His only defence against the Holocaust charge amounted to 'I did not hear about Auschwitz until now – I never knew of that before this trial. It's perfectly understandable and proper for one to be an anti-Semite, but to exterminate women and children is so extraordinary, it's hard to believe. No defendant here wanted that'.[30]

To those of normal moral standards Streicher comes across as disgusting, perverted, and psychologically unbalanced, and one look at any *Der Stürmer* would confirm this thinking. Instead of hanging him it might have been more useful to lock him up in a psychiatric hospital and used him for study analysis to help others who showed similar signs of obsessive dangerous behaviour. He fell out with Göring over personal matters, but the fact that Hitler appeared to support him says much about Hitler's mentality.

NUREMBERG TRIAL PAPERS

In the Courtroom

The Nuremberg Trial papers can be found in many archives, and even in second-hand book shops and on the Amazon book website. They were printed under the authority of the Attorney-General by His Majesty's Stationery Office, London, 1946. They reflect what was said at the time and may be seen as sound recorded Oral History of that day. What must always be borne in mind, as mentioned in the previous section, is that it was a trial in which the defendants would lie or exaggerate to avoid execution or imprisonment. In talking to a medic like Goldensohn and his colleagues they might be tempted to feel freer in what they said, but in a formal court room faced by international judges, professional barristers, press observers and the public was a very different scenario. Even witnesses from the concentration camps or who suffered under the Gestapo or SD might exaggerate their suffering as an act of revenge. Although it is pertinent to add that such victims had no need to exaggerate what is now known today.

Nevertheless, these papers record the feelings and emotions of the 1946 trial, and with 80 years of historical research it is now easier to tell when a defendant is simply lying or casting the blame on the already dead. In terms of witnesses much more is now widely known than before, but some of their statements still remain eye-openers of the corruption and suffering caused by the Nazi regime which managed to dominate Germany. As an example, one selection chosen by this writer was from a female French victim.

Madame Claude Vaillant Couturier

She was asked to repeat the statement 'I swear to speak without hate or fear. To state the truth, all the truth'.[31] Her background was explored, and she was a Deputy in the Constituent Assembly and a Knight of the Legion of Honour. She was a 'somebody' and probably carefully selected for this reason. In filling in her background, she explained she was arrested by the police of Vichy France, as a suspected member of the resistance.[32] She was handed over to the German authorities in February 1941.[33] This is an immediate reminder that the Vichy controlled part of France worked alongside the Germans in a *danse macabre* which even led to the death of many Jews living in that part of divided France. The question of Vichy France was not part of the trial but caused many problems in France during and after the war. She was taken to the Santé prison in the German quarter and refused to sign their document. She bravely said she was not afraid of being shot, but the interrogator said that would be an easy way out, compared to what would happen to her. The interpreter told her she would be sent to a 'concentration camp in Germany, one never comes back from there'.[34]

She spent five months in that prison and mentioned the names of many prisoners, many of whom she knew had been badly tortured then executed. She was transported to Auschwitz in January 1943. When asked about fellow travellers there were some 230 French women, many of them intellectuals and schoolteachers. It included elderly women, cripples and the sick, and teenage girls. It was no surprise as she explained that many died not long after they arrived.

She was asked to describe a roll-call in February not long after they arrived. She replied with the following:

> In the morning at 3.30 the whole camp was awakened and sent out on the plain, whereas normally the roll-call was at the same time, but inside the camp. We remained out in front of the camp in the snow until five in the afternoon without any food. Then when the signal was given, we had to go through the door one by one, and we were struck in the back with a cudgel, each one of us, in order to make us run. Those who could not run, either because they were too old or too ill, were caught by a hook and taken to Block 25, 'waiting block' for the gas chamber. On that day 10 of the French women of our convoy were thus caught and taken to the waiting block. When all the internees were back in the camp, a party to which I belonged was organised to go and pick up the bodies of the dead which were scattered over the plain as on a battlefield. We carried to the yard of Block 25 the dead and the dying without distinction, and they remained there stacked in the courtyard.[35]

This roll-call of having to stand from the middle of the night and virtually all day in the cold and snow without food or water and be rewarded by a cudgel blow is simply terrible to think about. In a novel it would hardly be believed, but it happened, which was why she was asked to describe that day. The motive for this mass torture can only be conjectured, it could have been a day off for most of the guards, or a means of disposing of the weak; no one can be certain.

She described how a young brave woman called Annette Épaux tried to take a drink to those suffering in the yard, was caught and thrown in to join those waiting their death. She also pointed out that if a Jewish internee turned up for any sudden roll-call without shoes, they were automatically sent to Block 25. She described the rate of infections and even the process of disinfection could be fatal, the lack of food, the punishment with blows and beatings. She described the treatment of newly arrived Jews. Her references to 'Block 25' evince a sense of horror in the reader's mind.

Eventually a few of their original number left Auschwitz but only to go to Ravensbrück where they had to go for a gynaecological examination with dirty instruments which meant infection spread rapidly.[36] After some roll-calls names were called out and they were never seen again.

This lady's evidence took a long time to give and there are pages of it in the Trial notes in small print. She somehow survived a place which made Hades feel like a holiday camp, and she was now giving evidence of her time there less than a year after she regained her freedom. One lengthy answer from her was quoted above, but it would take half the space of this book to give more. In the contents page she falls under the heading of 'Oral Evidence', which given the time space between imprisonment and the time of the trial was undoubtedly true, and this is supported by the now known information of these camps. This form of Oral History is invaluable to any reader because through these words it is the same as being transported back by a time space capsule to a place where we would rather not be and return in the hope it could never be repeated. Many Germans were horrified when this type of evidence was made public, but it was the result of the tyrannical and evil ideology of the Nazi regime so many (but not all) had accepted as the way forward.

It is interesting reading the many books written about the trial, especially those who took notes at the time. Many defendants were hanged, some imprisoned, and a few released. Some of these studies allow today's reader to see inside the minds of some of these defendants, and since many of these studies are based on Oral History, they carry more weight. One of the more interesting statements made for this writer was by François de Menthon who closed the French prosecution case stating:

> Who can say that I have a clean conscience; I am without fault? To use different weights and measures is abhorred by God … If this criminality had been accidental; if Germany had been forced into war, if war crimes had been committed only in the excitement of combat, we might question ourselves in the light of the Scriptures. But the war was prepared and deliberated long in advance, and upon the very last day it would have been easy to avoid it without sacrificing any of the legitimate interests of the German people. The atrocities were perpetrated during the war, not under the influence of a mad passion nor of a warlike anger nor of an avenging resentment, but as a result of cold calculation, of perfectly conscious methods, of a pre-existing doctrine.[37]

That pre-existing doctrine was Nazism projected by the autocracy of Adolf Hitler, and the warning of history is that such autocrats can and are rising again.

Chapter Five

Some Autobiographies

INTRODUCTION

This chapter moves solely into the area of reminiscent history which if sound can be as good and as interesting as Oral History. For many people the events they lived through have never left them, as if they happened yesterday. A few kept notes or logbooks, but for most people it was a matter of memory recall. As noted in this chapter's introduction when it comes to autobiographies, their value as a form of Oral History can be tested against the facts of history and by the judgement of the reader. For this writer who has read history for over 50 years, has written many history books, has sometime quoted them as evidence of the day, but has always paid attention to the validity of what has been written, they are unquestionably of more value than biographies, (unless they contain diary notes or letters by the subject of their study or written by a top professional) which can sometimes be valuable, but others descend to a form of hagiography. Even some autobiographies, especially those written by senior commanders can be sound, but their work often becomes a vehicle for self-justification, forms of apologia, and even for building up their public reputation. It is possible to mention a few but discretion warns otherwise.

From the autobiographies this writer has selected one German and one British fighter pilot, and three frontline soldiers. Each time facts which could be checked, were explored, and attention focused on possible exaggerations or deliberate evasions. There was also the test of truthfulness, looking for moments when the writer was self-denigrating about his own behaviour or reactions. Some of the selected admitted being scared stiff, having long or short-term breakdowns, others admitting to theft, one even landing up in prison for this crime. One of the British frontline soldiers experienced the immediate after-effects of the bombing of Dresden and was ashamed of being British, and for a short time joined the Communist Party.

One thing they had in common was their various experiences in the strife of war which had left indelible marks on their memories which they have been prepared to share with the next generation. In this sense, as a form of oral history, they are important. For many readers these works are more interesting to read than formal textbooks, and they might encourage an interest in history which, as stated time and time again, we shall repeat the disasters of the past if we neglect them.

GEOFFREY WELLUM

FIGHTER PILOT

This is an autobiographical account of the war years of a young boy called Geoffrey Wellum who walked out of his Forest Gate School, Snaresbrook aged just over 17, having applied to the Air Ministry because he wanted to become a fighter pilot. He was one of the youngest to serve in this capacity, and it is startling today to recall how many teenagers joined the ranks of battle during the two World Wars. An elderly French resistance fighter once explained when in the late 1930s how critical he was of teenagers' behaviour at night outside the clubs, but how these same youngsters died fighting in the resistance against the Nazi occupiers; youth was vital during conflict. Wellum saw action in the Battle of Britain, covered convoys, including Operation *Pedestal* (Malta), attacked Nazi bomber fleets and gave cover to RAF bombers attacking Nazi areas in France. He worked and fought for three years without any break and had to be treated for sinusitis [infected nasal passages] and battle fatigue, but he stayed in the RAF long after the war was finished.

Over fifty years later Wellum was approached by the historian James Holland and the outcome was an autobiography entitled *First Light*. Wellum admitted in his prologue it was reminiscent writing and that he kept no diary.[1] However, it struck this writer that there was plenty of real oral history in many places, and several times Wellum in his text referred to notes which he had kept from time to time, noting 'I am sitting outside the dispersal tents on the far side of the airfield writing these notes' and 'How quickly a pen going back and forth across a page consumes time. I try to put the events of the past few months into some sort of order, but I find it very difficult'.[2] As an historian this writer has read many autobiographies but this fell into that small category where it feels the author of this biography was not only using notes from the day, but even where he reminisces it is accurate and truthful, not only about events, but how he felt.

He admits it was not an easy time and that he often wondered if he would fail, and he was warned that he would fail his flying lessons and was threatened with being deployed to ground staff. Several times he was accused of mere average flying, writing of a conversation in which a senior officer told him, 'At the moment, Wellum, we haven't much time for you. You are existing here on a knife edge. Now go away and think what I said'.[3] At times, evening during his training he had admitted he was often scared and prone to panic, writing 'A bloody fine pilot you, I don't think. Well, I can't stay up here all night so let's try again. Help me God, please don't let me do a Laurie, I'm a bit frightened and lonely up here in the dark'.[4] This sense of being terrified, panicking and calling upon God for help is frequent throughout his account, it is open and honest and has the ring of absolute truth, as it is not mentioned just once and passed over, but an insight which permeates his whole text. Later in his account he wrote 'As I watch the 109, I now know the meaning of the word fear, stark staring fear, the sort of fear that few people possibly ever experience. I find myself yelling at him. Goodness knows why, I suppose it helps'.[5] Even near the end of writing he adds 'everything inside me seems to turn itself into a knot and stark fear grips me. Will it be my turn today to get the chop ? Please God, help me to cope'.[6] It is not the style of many similar works for the author to admit to such feelings and to be so consistent in admitting he was always so terrified.

As a young teenager during a social session when training they discussed the dangers of their future, writing that 'the thoughts of the possibility of being killed is duly worrying or upsetting. One just ignores it. Each is convinced that it cannot possibly happen to him'.[7] This feeling of personal survival rings many bells for all of us in peace and war and has been mentioned by many, a common human experience. Later, in the heat of battle, lost in clouds, landing at night on a fog-bound airfield at Manston, the possibility of his own death passed through his mind, but he survived the war and died aged 96 on 18 July 2018.

He watched with horror his friends being killed, thinking of them still strapped to their seats somewhere under the English Channel. Waiting with concern for others who were disturbingly late back from a mission and being horrified by the fighting thousands of feet above the earth's surface. His humanity comes through when he describes in a dogfight, planes being shot down, planes crashing downwards, and added 'Well, he may be a Hun, but I wouldn't wish a death like that on anybody'.[8]

Throughout his book there is a glaring honesty in his account. It could be argued that it is well-written for this sense of conveying reality, but he does it by denigrating his own conduct, his self-deprecating views, his sense of fear while as a youngster he felt like others that he would survive, but soon doubting this hope. He admitted that he was concerned about his flying abilities and the time it took for him to learn navigating at a high altitude, and more to the point, he does not just admit his sense of panic and fear, but this stays a dominant feature of his work.

When leading figures of generals and admirals write their autobiographies they are often focused on the strategies and tactics of the war, the justification for their views, and they can be assessed against the work of able historians. For the fighting man in the air, on land, and at sea what has to come through to the reader is that sense of oral history, which is when it reflects an integrity, which can, more often than not, be found in their personal feelings, attitudes, which must reflect a reality which the reader can recognise by instinct.

ULRICH STEINHILPER

GERMAN FIGHTER PILOT

Interestingly in contrast to the above autobiography of Geoffrey Wellum above is a German autobiography written in 1989 by a Messerschmidt Bf109 pilot called Ulrich Steinhilper who was two-three years older than Wellum. Both books provide insights into the teenagers and often very young men who fought the duels in the skies as fighter pilots. They do not reflect true Oral history, but they come close, as they are reminiscent reflections written by men with time to reflect, and they were both active during the war, albeit on different sides, and in the case of Steinhilper he includes many letters written at the time.[9] By the time of writing his autobiography Steinhilper was fully aware that the Nazi regime was corrupt but he still faithfully indicates his youthful adherence to Hitler.

Steinhilper flew some 150 sorties and destroyed some Spitfires on the ground and one or two in aerial combat and was regarded as an ace. However, he was shot down over Canterbury in Kent in October 1940, shipped to Canada as a PoW and twice tried to escape. He was released in 1946 and had a successful postwar career, dying in 2009.

Most of his book is about his family life and growing up in Germany during the interbellum years. He explained that his father, who had fought in the First World War felt that 'Germany had been stripped naked by the Treaty of Versailles' and Hitler was offering drive and hope.[10] He also recalled that whereas the Weimer Republic had cut government-employed worker salaries by 10 per cent Hitler had made radical changes. An historian with the benefit of hindsight would point out that this was Hitler's drive in 1933 to booster his popularity, but Steinhilper just adds that this made Hitler popular.[11] He also commented on the power of the Nuremberg Rallies, but pointing out that if he and his friends were expected to parade it took away their 'flying hours'.[12] His father in 1938 was a headteacher and there was some tussle by other Party Members that they would be better at the post (every headteacher's nightmare). Steinhilper admitted that when he turned up in his Luftwaffe uniform with wings this settled the problem.[13] Later in a letter home he wrote about the news of the alleged assassination of Hitler (the *Buergerbräukeller* Plot) writing that 'I was happy that it turned out OK. To me it is clear that England is behind this'.[14] He never shies away from his support of Hitler, relating how he felt at the time, not at the time of writing in the postwar era.

The autobiography reaches the war years over halfway through the text. He made the interesting observation that in the war against Poland it was popularly reported the Polish planes were destroyed before they could take off. Instead, he recalled they put up a stubborn fight, and it was just that their aircraft were not that good.[15] This sounds closer to the truth because many Poles made it to Britain to serve as pilots where they were highly respected and admired for their bravery. As was the case with most pilots the need to wait for the call to action was numbing, writing to his mother (24 September 1939) 'we lead a sorry life, waiting is probably worse than war'.

When the war against Britain started it soon dawned on him was going to be 'a hard fight ...when we first saw the Hurricanes and Spitfires attacking our Stukas...it was very clear that we were up against very tenacious opposition'.[16] He wrote to his mother (11 August 1940) 'Today I had four missions. Three of us shot down a Bristol Blenheim which was about to attack one of our air-sea rescue planes'.[17] In his main text this caused him to wonder 'what kind of people we were fighting'.[18] The war was growing bitter and frenetic and despite international agreements both sides broke the rules either by individual choice or command, based on suspicion and the need for victory. He admitted that they were all suffering from *Kanalkrankheit* (Channel Sickness) brought about by stress and fatigue, which was undoubtedly also felt by their opposition.[19] This was not helped by watching a man descending by a parachute on fire and dropping more and more quickly by the second.[20]

This autobiography appears in many ways to be a totally honest reflection on his youth in Nazi Germany and as a Luftwaffe pilot. It is part of 'memory heritage' and appears to be both candid and honest, and the saved family letters help to give confidence in its integrity.

REGINALD CAMBRIDGE

ARMY PRIVATE

In stark contrast to Wellum's autobiography is that of a Londoner, Reginald Cambridge as it is also the life of a young boy but who joined the army as a private, sometimes referred to as a squaddie. It is a private publication which was printed in 2015.[21] Within the text he copies part of a diary he kept, but it is not that which makes it oral history, but his reminiscent thoughts are evidently honest and reflect the truth of his life and days. This is substantiated by his open admittance he was before a Military Court three times based on theft (he called the thieves 'tea leaves'), and on charges of absent without leave [AWOL]. Initially, he had wanted to 'fly a fighter plane, zooming around the heavens' but the recruiting office were not interested and feeling 'deflated' he turned to the army.[22] He had been an apprentice butcher and joined the LDV (Local Defence Volunteer) later known as the Home Guard. By doing so it healed a rift with his father, but he made no further comment on this because this account was evidently written for the benefit of the family and close friends. The fact that he pulls no punches about his misbehaviour is a sure sign that it is an honest account.

In the army he found in the barracks young men who were a mixture of thieves and who disregarded rules and regulations, but who would one day fight in North Africa, Sicily, and Italy. This is a reminder of the Duke of Wellington during the Peninsular War looking at same recently arrived raw recruits saying, 'I don't know what the enemy think, but by God, they scare me'. This autobiography is a sharp reminder of the way the pressure of the Nazi threat encouraged the various recruiting offices to take all and sundry, including potential criminals and often ignoring false birth dates.

While Britain was defending its own shores in the air and soldiers on the channel coastline, at this time there were no British troops in the war zone, and so young Cambridge between military training found himself and his 'mates' filling in as farm labourers cracking the joke that the PBI (the Poor Bloody Infantry) had some meaning.[23] Meanwhile there were murmurings they were going to be sent abroad, and being mere privates and not being senior officers, there was constant gossip of where, but when their convoy left the Clyde they realised their main gossip of North Africa had been correct, describing on their arrival a discovery of a new world, the heat, smells, colours, making this a new experience as from their social class few would have been abroad before. Cambridge spends many pages describing the nature of the fighting in a matter-of-fact way, describing the incidents which happened within his area and giving space to his group catching a chicken to eat.[24] He described a personal encounter with a German soldier who slightly injured him with a bayonet before he shot him with his rifle. His description has no emotions, and it reads more like a modern traffic accident report. This gives the reader the impression that he had emotionally detached himself from past events, although he mentions there were vicious battles, and in Sicily he seemed more concerned about the sores caused by the straps of what he was carrying and the smells of the volcano Etna. He mentioned a dying new friend of 18 calling for his mother, and later in the text a German called for his *Mutter*, meeting Black Americans who were only regarded as supply troops. It was in Sicily he and a few friends taking an unofficial holiday, nearly missing the crossing for mainland Italy in an act of being Absent Without Leave, for which he lost 27 days of pay and ten days of field punishment which meant digging toilets.

He found after the move to the toe of Italy quiet moments where he was more concerned about ridding his clothes of lice. He admitted he and his mates became good at missing parades and they all loved playing cards. He nearly had more disciplinary trouble over stolen cigarettes but fortunately lied his way out from the problem. He was accepted for Commando training despite the fact that he had been considered an undesirable because of his offences and detention time, or that may have even been the reason for his selection. He returned to England for a break and spent most of his time organising parties for young women. After the German collapse he was in Germany he joined the Control Commission of Germany, the CCG, which they referred to as 'Charlie Chaplin's Grenadiers'.[25] He was demobbed and returned home to find life in south London boring and quickly returned to the army, later left, and rejoined again. He was made a sergeant, then back to private on what was technically his third army entry and then finally back to sergeant before he retired in 1971. He found his tours encompassed Malaya, the Netherlands, West Germany, Singapore, Hong Kong, and Northen Ireland.

This book is about a very ordinary everyday soldier who treated the army like a job, more interesting, with generally better pay than at home. He was again in trouble when a civilian prisoner escaped, but he left the service with a good record. It comes across, even during the war years, as a boring time, just the need to survive and enjoy life at any given opportunity, even if it meant breaking the rules. He was the very ordinary man making the most of a job which was a mixture of danger, boredom, strict regulations, and seeking some fun even if it meant breaking the rules. His personal disclosures are honest and in terms of reminiscence, driving it close to oral history, he relates the reality of life in the army for many very ordinary people.

ALEX BOWLBY

RIFLEMAN

When the author Alex Bowlby died in 2005 the obituary in *The Times* stated he 'will be remembered for a book that gave one of the most honest and vivid accounts of the British soldier's experience during the Second World War'.[26] When this book was finished it proved difficult to find a publisher, but has since been reprinted several times, with some commentators seeing a hint of a Wilfred Owen in the way he viewed war. John Keegan wrote that this book 'belongs to the genre of military literature known as 'a voice from the ranks'.[27] It is a book of reminiscences from a man with bitter firsthand experience of war, and his details of singular incidents and events are so detailed it comes close to an on-the-spot commentary. He truthfully admits that some of the detailed information of events he picked up from his fellow soldiers, and that he once tried to keep a 'sketchy diary'.[28] It was not a long-term reflection as he drafted the first copy of his experiences in 1947 when he was still in a state of shock. In 1955 he had a breakdown, which in putting this into writing showed his willingness to open up on his thinking and experiences. This reminiscent autobiography is so openly written exposing his deepest feelings, the nature of the friends he fought with, the description of the war so realistic, the reader could feel they were there, which is not a literary gift, but the honest insight of a man who was there, making it a form of Oral History.

It is written in such a way the humour and fear are mixed together, fear not just of the enemy but fear of disgrace for being seen as a coward. and often the depression of the ordinary frontline soldier is made noticeably clear. It involves not just the bitter conflict in Italy, but the author mentions such matters as the usual criticisms and complaints of the fighting soldier about decisions made by senior command. Bowlby raises the subject of personal fear, the sense of panic of not being able to cope, and even the embarrassing question of desertion which was rife in Italy. It also underlines the way military conflict brings different men together forming a bond between them as strong as a sound family. Later Bowlby considered volunteering as a stretcher bearer, a friend said it was a worthwhile job, but he would have to leave their unit, which changed his mind as he desperately depended on their friendship.[29]

Unusually it is not until halfway through the book that the author Bowlby exposes his own background which in itself is a fascinating account. This moment of reflection occurred when he was attending a funeral of recently killed comrades led by the padre, who had spoken the well-known lines 'I lift up mine eyes to the hills from whence cometh my strength'. Bowlby looked up to the hills behind the padre where his friends had been shot and reflected on how close he had been to being killed.[30] Within a few lines of relating this experience he thought of how he had joined the army in the first place. He had an unusual background for a private because he came from a public school from where the military authority expected officers, but failed the selection tests, having special trouble with the interviewing psychiatrist, and from this writer's perspective he probably alienated himself because of his open personality. Later in the book he noted that when officers knew he had the same public school background as themselves, it made relationships somewhat delicate.[31] It was probably his open personality which made it easy to befriend those from the working classes as he fought alongside them and became one of them.

When his battalion arrived in Capua (a city in the Province of Caserta in southern Italy) it was his twentieth birthday, and he was not the youngest. After the war he visited the cemetery and noted the vast majority of graves were of men aged between 18 and 20 years. His sense of humour throughout the book is catching. He, like many others, smoked a pipe but his had a huge bowl and unusual shape, with some telling him it looked like a two-inch mortar, some saw it as a saxophone, and others a lavatory bowl. When a Corporal Baker saw it, he said that if the Germans 'saw my pipe they'd pack it in'.[32] Several times he lost his pipe and one time cried, but it was so recognisable it was often returned when found by others. Throughout this book he and his comrades found a sense of emotional sustenance in joking which was not just graveside humour. Many who served on the frontline would recognise this as a feature of life which kept up the spirits of men who were constantly facing boredom then dreadful danger. As one First World War soldier said army life was 90 per cent sheer tedium and boring, and 10 per cent too much excitement and fright.

Bowlby uses many first-person conversations, naturally drawn from memory, but to the historian's ear they sound real and highly likely. We may all reflect on conversations from decades ago, but while not able to reconstruct them word for word, the major essence can be reproduced. When an older comrade told Bowlby not to worry that he would look after him, Bowlby replied 'It's funny, you know. I feel excited and afraid at the same time', and 'we grinned at one another'.[33] Strict oral history often demands accounts written at the time, recorded interviews or conversations, and films. When on tape for any reason most people tend to be more wary of what they say, and it could be argued that remembered and reconstructed conversations from those in the actual conflict may be more exact when they have nothing to hide. On a recorded tape or film, a soldier may say he feels confident in their orders and not worried by his duties. To his mates he might later claim the 'captain's timing of attack is plain stupid, and I am scared witless'.

Emotions and feelings are important and when conveyed in reminiscent oral history they not only relate a truth, but a psychological issue which sometimes results in long-term post-traumatic stress which Bowlby appeared to have postwar to a limited extent. This writer remembers his father inviting a friend home every Guy Fawkes night because he needed company when the night was full of noise, some of which sounded like explosions. When asked why by his curious young son, he explained he had been a soldier and wounded by a shell. Bowlby conveys this sense of deep emotion as he passed through Cassino, where he saw burnt out tanks, wooden crosses topped with coal-scuttle helmets, but above all the smell: 'the sour-sweet stench of rotting flesh…instinctively I realised I was smelling my own kind, and not animals…the unseen dead, unconsecrated dead assume a most terrifying power. Their protest filled the truck. We avoided one another's eyes'.[34] On another occasion they walk by a dead German with a severed leg at the hip and with staring eyes, and 'we walked past him as if our legs were made of glass'.[35]

No one wanted to be a coward, and for many this was yet another fear. The German troops in Italy were of the highest standard, led by highly competent officers, headed by the able Field Marshal Kesselring. Amongst the most feared troops were their paratroopers, and when Bowlby and his comrades were told to 'debus' because some of these paratroopers were still around, Bowlby noted 'For a moment no one moved…nobody wanted to meet them'.[36] Bowlby then described how he crawled towards a gap in the hedge to peep up the road.

The essence of fear dominated their lives. Throughout their time they were constantly having to dig shelters and slit trenches in hard rock-filled land to find shelter from incoming mortar and shell attacks. Being too close to the explosion could mean death or life-changing injuries, and there was the constant fear of shrapnel. Later in the text Bowlby would always associate these attacks with someone calling out for stretcher bearers. There was no safe response except to dig a hole or find some shelter in Mother Earth, but this did not stop a shell or mortar bomb landing on you, and a number of times he mentions men who had never had any belief in God found themselves praying. Shakespeare caught this in his play *The Tempest* when the ship is sinking, and the sailors call out 'all is lost, all is lost, to prayer, to prayer'. In the first book in this chapter the reader will recall the fighter pilot Wellum was forever holding conversations and pleading for help from the Almighty. At one time Bowlby asked God not to let him die 'until I have held a woman'.[37] Later his wish to 'to have a woman' was fulfilled by Italian women trying to make some money for food. As Wellum longed for a walk in the English countryside, so Bowlby heard larks singing between explosions, which for him 'made war seem sillier than ever'.[38] Sometimes the sheer noise of a raging battle would 'hammer his nerves to jelly'.[39] Other times it was the silence which scared him, always thinking something was about to happen.[40]

The sense of fear was continuous, and it tended to lead Bowlby to moments of deep depression, sometimes induced by illness and more often than not by the way of life, wondering whether there was any light at the end of the tunnel.[41] At times he experienced waves of nausea which led to the state of depression. He was honest enough to admit at times that he simply cried and cursed the war.

As with many of other people who are under orders, authority is often challenged by the rank and file. When told they were about to attack a village before the Germans pulled out, Bowlby recalled a man called Gibson calling out 'Sod that, why can't we let them get out first'.[42] On reading this outburst it could be argued that the situation meant the Germans would lose men, but if standing there like Gibson, he would have made sense. He was warned that these are orders so no one could quarrel.

There is also that deep fear in many that no one wants to be regarded as a coward. On one occasion Bowlby considered moving away but recalled 'I was more concerned about not running away. The mixture of fear and excitement…it was like sitting in a boxing-ring, waiting for the bell'.[43] There is no doubt that the reputation of the 'Teds' (that is *Tedeschi*, which was Italian for the Germans) was intense. The need not to disgrace himself became yet another fear which dogged him from time to time.

Several times Bowlby mentioned the unmentionable, of people fleeing, the deserters who fighting for their lives in a potentially beautiful country with an attractive climate and friendly people, realised it would be more attractive deserting in Italy than in a North African desert.

He also describes a comrade searching amongst corpses for watches. Running away from the bitter conflict crossed Bowlby's mind, after one heated battle writing 'And if I do get out, I thought, I'll desert. Anything's better than this'.[44]

He rarely commented on the Germans, seeing them just as the deadly foe, but having a meal in a farmhouse where the Germans had just been he thought about them, adding 'The war was bad enough for us. What must it be like for them? Always retreating, and knowing, most of them, that they have no hope of winning?'[45] He did note later that when the watching Germans saw them burying their dead, they did not use this as an opportunity to attack.

This autobiography first prepared in 1947 feels so close to reality, even to a professional historian, and while recognising it is based on reminiscences it is almost as good, if not better than many other forms of Oral History.

VICTOR GREGG

A Frontline Soldier

In the fifth selected autobiography there was a degree of uncertainty as to its value as sound memory recollection because the book was so wide ranging. On the back of the publication the historian James Holland described this autobiography 'as action packed as any fiction and yet this is no novel…his is a truly an astonishing story'. This writer read it again but not as a tale, but as a serious retelling of the man's lifetime, and thought that even if there were a few question marks they were totally insignificant compared to the bulk of the book which came across as the author's account of his life.[46] Gregg was born in 1919, grew up on the streets of London as a working class boy, joined the army in 1937, released in 1946, and the final part of the book deals with his ups and downs and marital issues in the postwar period. He died just three days short of his 102nd birthday in 2021. It is not just a war diary, which is the most fascinating part, but could be seen as a social history, a young London lad driven by an adrenaline rush through most of his life. On his birthday on 15 October 1937, having lost another job, he watched a parade in Whitehall and was invited to have a tea and a bun by a uniformed soldier with 'more stripes on his uniform than a zebra', and landed up with the King's shilling having signed on to join the Rifle Brigade and never had the cup of tea.[47] Throughout the book his sense of humour frequently emerges.

After basic training and with his new 'pals' he found himself off to India by ship, and from there to Palestine, in both places finding different forms of action. In January 1940, with the Second World War having started he found himself in the Citadel in Cairo. Here he soon found himself at war with the Italians, and he and his mates heard about the bombing of London which infuriated them almost making the fight personal. He wrote 'many a poor, hapless Eyetie felt the agony of a bayonet going in, wielded by an enraged Rifleman who had just got a letter from home bearing bad news'.[48] They had new recruits join them including the actor David Niven and Quintin Hogg (later Lord Hailsham) and in his book Gregg always describes the battles he fought in with revealing detail. In one battle he watched the Italian General Bergonzoli and some senior officers surrender. Later they found they were against Rommel's *Afrika Korps*, writing 'a nasty shock was on the horizon'.[49] He related to the time, which many soldiers have recorded, when some of his comrades met the 'Krauts, and instead of doing each other mortal danger' they arranged an exchange of Schnapps for English cigarettes.[50] Later he also records the moments when a brief ceasefire was called when the wounded could be brought into safety.[51]

Then as a small group they were virtually given a holiday to South Africa transporting PoWs by ship where they were welcomed and entertained beyond their wildest expectations, returning to North Africa in October 1941. He describes many battles he witnessed, especially the pain and suffering he saw, there are no romantic streaks in his descriptions. He saw men being killed, writing 'we watched helpless while the 22nd Armoured Brigade was blown to pieces attempting to advance over dead-flat terrain into the mouths of waiting guns'.[52] His responses are very human and although he was evidently a competent and willing soldier there is no romanticising about the nature of war and its barbarities.

He had however been identified as proficient and a survivor, and he was sent off for what he called to meet 'cloak and dagger stuff'. He was sent off to Telekabir Barracks where he was taken by a 'Red cap who looked more like a tailor's dummy than a member of His Majesty's forces'.[53] He was questioned about the desert and asked if he knew this place or that and how to get there and was soon told about his new task. He had been seconded to the Long-Range Desert Group (LRDG) more as a courier who knew his way about the desert. When he looked back at his time basically serving as a driver across the desert wastes, he wrote that 'I never fired a shot in anger. My mates back in the Rifle Brigade were being slaughtered at places called Gazala and Knightsbridge. My main problem was enemy aircraft'.[54]

On his return to his unit which was heading for the Alamein line, he had had his leg pulled as being a skiver which he took in good humour. They heard the news that their favourite officer General 'Strafer' Gott had been shot down while travelling by air, and Montgomery was to take his place. Gregg's account of the battles is direct and realistic adding 'we were all shit-scared and trying not to show it', which in both his language and descriptions reveals a high degree of veracity in his account of events.[55]

His next turn of fate was when he described his time as what he called a 'birdman' and he became a paratrooper. He was due to be dropped in the invasion of Sicily, but he was one of the lucky ones because his flight was stopped in time, as the failure to tell the navy what was happening caused their guns to shoot down their own planes and gliders and hundreds of men were killed by their own side. Later he landed up sailing to Taranto as part of the invasion of Italy and finding they were welcomed by ordinary Italian citizens. He described taking the Foggia airfields which was important as it gave the Allies a much-needed advantage. In places the going was tough against the German opposition, and he was frank enough to admit for a time he 'went through a very bad phase of the shakes' but eventually overcame this understandable problem.[56]

When the news came that they were heading for home he described the time they stood on the deck of the transport ship when 'men who would normally be laughing and joking were quietly leaning on the rails, staring into the distance. What thoughts were passing through their minds was anyone's guess,' saying little more, leaving the reader to speculate his thinking which may have been about lost comrades and what their next battle was and where.[57] The first was to be a parachute drop near Caen, but it was stopped as news came through the Germans were in the dropping zone. Later he boarded another flight for the Falaise battle but after circling the area that too was abandoned. His next flight was to be dropped in Arnhem, the disastrous *Market Garden* Operation providing some interesting descriptions of the battle but where he was captured and imprisoned.

The rest of his war account was about his time in a German PoW labour camp outside Dresden where he tried and failed to escape. His description of the Camp Commandant was balanced as he treated his prisoners with a degree of respect. He saw the after-effects of the major bombing raid on Dresden in which the PoWs had to help. The 'barbarity' of the raid shook him, and he wrote 'for myself I felt ashamed that, being British, I was associated with this immorality'.[58]

He escaped because of this mayhem and met the Russian forces surging west. He found the Ukrainian forces 'behaved in a very gruesome way' and 'the Russians showed no compassion'.[59] After the war he was questioned about this time with the Soviet forces as postwar there was a growing paranoia as the Cold War was starting. He became for a time a member of the British Communist Party, and the final part of his book details his life in the postwar years, where his first marriage folded and he married again, supporting his need for the adrenaline rush with sport.

When he left the army in 1946 his certificate of service recorded the following: 'During an exceedingly colourful career this rifleman has served long and continuous periods in active operations with front line units. He is an individual of great courage, capable of applying himself best to a task when the need is greatest'.[60]

Pre-war and the post-war years make interesting reading for those curious about social history, but his life in the army saw him in India, the Middle East, North Africa (even South Africa for a time), Italy, Arnhem, the experience of being a PoW and meeting with the Soviets. As noted in this chapter's introduction when it comes to autobiographies, their value as a form of Oral History can be tested against the facts of history and by the judgement of the reader. For this writer who has read history for over 50 years, has written many history books, and spent too much time in the archives, this autobiography scores 95 per cent, even after a second reading.

Chapter Six

Final Observations

As noted in the Preface, history is an important subject not because it repeats itself but offers many warnings from the past which are often all too pertinent to the age in which we currently live, with the rise again of autocracy, the influence of wealth, political power, and the possible re-occurrence of major wars. For many people history is just a school subject studied by a few at university. Many find the subject boring and their only knowledge of the past century tends to come from films based on the two World Wars. Films are enjoyable because from the comfort and safety of the armchair it is a means of being where the action took place. Oral History written or recorded at the time or reminiscent history written not long after events can do this, making history much more interesting because it is read by those who were there and not through the eyes of a film director. Oral history is slightly more important than the heritage of memory, but both can be subject to subtle changes for which the general reader and historian must be alert. Even when changes may have been made it carries its own value as to why it was deemed necessary to make alterations.

Chapter One relates to the personal experience of listening to those who were involved or saw a particular event are of interest both to the media and the courtroom. Hearing about a person's reactions, thoughts and feelings of a major event offers a high degree of understanding and knowledge. The various publications are mainly based on Oral History, but some are evidently reminiscent memory, which can be just as sound but must be judged carefully.

There are many books based on this subject, a few with question marks, but most offering witnesses from the past. The previous century was a period of global conflict with the Second World War being the most prominent because of its ramifications. There are books based on the views of soldiers, sailors, airmen, and some on the reaction of everyday citizens, almost reading like committee books. When read the major lessons comes through, especially that the causes of conflict must be identified so they do not happen again.

Chapter Two delved into the personal family letters which were German, American, and British in origin, and because they are family letters there is no reason to doubt their validity. They take us inside the mind of the writer, many dwelling on the importance of family and the need to survive. Unchanged letters and diaries written at the time are a sound form of Oral History

The letters of Heinrich Himmler are simply 'mind-boggling' as the organiser of the death camps comes across as a deeply emotional person, thus the sub-title of *The Banality of Evil*. There are letters from two major commanders revealing their personalities, often proving the historical textbooks correct. One series of letters from a senior German officer and another set from a German foot soldier on the Eastern Front deeply concerned about his family at home. From the senior German officer, we learn some details about the fighting in North Africa and his attitudes towards his Italian allies, and even towards the British enemy. The one factor the *Afrika Korps* officer and the man on the Eastern Front share is the reader's perception that both places were a form of Hades, which contrast with the letters from George Orwell, which despite the tensions, were written in relative comfort. These letters take us back to a time of pain and sorrow, and deep into the thinking processes of the writers and their families.

Chapter Three is important because it contains a study of nine diaries of interest, from wide ranging national sources, including British, German, Italian, a White Russian and a German-Jew. Two are from important governmental figures, in Germany and Italy, a German diplomat, a German Judge, the most senior British General, and two senior Civil Servants working in Buckingham Palace and 10 Downing Street, even though they knew it was against the rules to keep diaries. They also include the diary of a Russian émigrée happily living in Berlin and the lengthy diaries of a German Jew who was a well-known academic and survived the persecution because he was married to a so-called Aryan German. They are all very different but have much to offer in terms of when and why they were written, and they have been selected because they are mainly genuine, unlike Hitler's Diary which was eventually seen as fake, although supported for a time by the historian Hugh Trevor-Roper.

Field Marshal Alanbrooke's diary starts with his role in the Battle of France but becomes of stronger interest when he is appointed by Churchill as Chief of the Imperial General Staff (CIGS). The diary clearly shows the stress and strain of leading a nation in the time of war, the relationship between military and political leaders in the British democracy, the frustrations between the British and Americans over strategy, amongst many other features of 'life at the top of military command'. There is no doubting the diary's validity because of Brooke's embarrassing critical views of Brooke about the postwar-worshipped Churchill, who chose Brooke because he needed strong minded men in support.

Mussolini's son-in-law and Foreign Minister Galeazzo Ciano's diary may have had a few redactions in places, but mainly when he was sacked and sidelined in the Vatican, and even these inform the reader of his thinking at the time. This diary offers many insights into Italy's role in the pre-war years and during the Second World War, including Mussolini's plans and ambitions. Ciano's diary in many ways reflects the views of many Italians during this era. He started as an enthusiastic supporter of Mussolini in hope of returning to the Roman grandeur of the distant past, he became less enthusiastic as the Nazi-Germans started to take more control as Italy became more reliant on their major ally. He became involved with Mussolini's fall from power and was eventually executed during Mussolini's brief time as controller of his small puppet state.

The diary of the German Jewish Professor Klemperer was kept day by day and hidden by friends and is a glowing example of Oral History indicating his thinking day by day. His entries range from commenting on Goebbels and the Nazi state to major events and his everyday shopping expeditions. He never conceals his hatred of the Nazi system, on the other hand there is a sense of genuine relief when he talks of shopkeepers and other ordinary Germans who are pleasant to him. It is noteworthy the way he and fellow inhabitants of Dresden tended to live off rumours about what was happening not only in their city but the wider world. He does not hide his feelings, noting that he had gone from being a well-known 'professor to a hunted animal'. The diary does not finish in 1945, and he welcomed the Soviet saviours but in time changed his mind. Three massive volumes constitute a long and determined reading, but as Oral History it provides numerous insights into everyday life in Germany from an academic determined to survive and write about what he experienced.

Goebbels' diaries are better known, a man who was determined to be important in life and by worshipping Hitler managed for a time to be seen as a leading component of the Nazi regime. He makes many errors of judgement which could have been cleared up a few weeks or months later, but he did not seem concerned about such blunders, which gives his diary entries a sense of being reliable Oral History. His reputation for propelling the Germans forward in anti-Semitism, anti-Church, and seeing themselves as a superior race is evident in his diaries. The diaries also clearly indicate he was, apart from being obsessive about the Nazi regime, a liar and felt justified to be so. The diary is distasteful as was its author, and he managed to lead many Germans astray (but not all), even when the war was evidently lost his description of 'wonder weapons' gave some hope and confirmed the cynicism of others. As a piece of Oral History, it provides a unique insight into the Nazi mindset.

At the opposite end of the spectrum is the diary of a White Russian émigrée called Marie Vassiltchikov which is best described as a personal social diary. Because of her Russian upper-class Tsarist background, she was able to mix with some leading figures from Germany and elsewhere. She even came across Ciano whose diary is mentioned above, and she found him morally distasteful. She knew of some of the figures involved in the 20 July Plot and was worried for them, with some justification. She was an ardent Christian worshipper [Russian Orthodox], expressing concern at the bombing of Rome and Monte Cassino, over which Nazi propaganda revelled in the bad publicity for the Allies. She worked basically as a secretary with her shorthand helping her to keep a diary. Parts of the diary are missing, possibly from personal or even political choice, nevertheless, what has been left offers a variety of insights gleaned at the time. She gives insights into life in Berlin, not least some sound descriptions of living there during the bombing raids. Her diary can be described as homely or personal but provides a focus on life in Berlin.

A good deal of thought went into whether to include the diary of Otto Müller-Hill, a 59-year-old German Judge who started his diary in 1944 with a purpose in mind. He was an intelligent man who saw that disaster was encroaching Germany, and he needed his young son to see him in the best possible light. It was an effort for self-justification but raises the question as to whether it could be a preparation for his defence in a trial by the victors. He admitted keeping a diary was potentially dangerous, not least because he was highly critical of colleagues who persisted in believing in ultimate Nazi victory. He was one of those who was highly critical of the Nazi propaganda by Goebbels. On the encouraging side of the diary's validity is his personal bigotry coming to light. Although he stated he was against the murder of the Jews, (though he obviously had no idea of the immense numbers involved), he was evidently a racist, angry about drunken negroes dropping bombs. Given that amongst the victors would be the Americans he was angry and ranted about their conduct of war and how they fought. This diary is for the reader to judge, but it is included because it represented the thinking of an intelligent and well-educated middle-class German in 1944.

The diary of Sir Alan Lascelles, known as Tommy by close friends, is interesting Oral History not because he was at the centre of British Royal life as a private secretary, but because his sense of humour raises a smile. He relates an overheard joke about Montgomery, and about how he stopped King George VI changing the design of the Stalingrad silver sword of victory to be given to Stalin. Had he not persuaded the King otherwise Stalin would have been insulted. He reflects the tittle-tattle of the day as well as the events and current opinions. He agreed with others that de Gaulle was an ongoing problem, referred to the problems caused by chaining captured German soldiers at Dieppe, and mentioned the tragic incident at Bethnal Green Underground when hundreds were killed or injured in a crowd stampede. One of the more interesting aspects was when the diarist worked hard to stop Churchill and the King attending Normandy D-Day with all the manipulative arguments which were mustered by the prime minister.

Similar to the Lascelles' diary was that written by John Colville, Private Secretary in 10 Downing Street, the centre of British democratic power. He knew it was against the rules to keep a diary but persisted thinking that keeping a record was important for the future. He made errors of judgment on events, being critical about the news of German concentration camps, thinking it was nonsense stirred up against the enemy. Later, when their barbarity was exposed, there were no signs of his views being changed or redacted, making the diary feel secure for Oral History. He first served Neville Chamberlain and offers some interesting views on this Prime Minister, appeared suspicious of Churchill but when serving under him changed his mind and related some amusing anecdotes about Churchill and his sense of humour. As a young man he decided to leave Downing Street to be a pilot in the RAF, was soon recalled, returned to the RAF for D-Day Normandy, and promptly called back to Churchill's offices. He was evidently a sound man and one whom Churchill seemed to appreciate.

The final diary is complex with names that often have to be checked by professional historians. It was written by a person from a Prussian aristocratic background known as Ulrich von Hassell. He was, like most from his social caste, a strong-minded right-wing conservative who at first took to Hitler and the NSDAP probably because of the strains caused by the Treaty of Versailles on his beloved country. As the 1930s in Germany unravelled, he became more and more critical of the Nazi regime, not least he was horrified by the events of *Kristallnacht*. He thoroughly disliked his immediate boss Ribbentrop, and while ambassador to Italy fell out with Ciano mentioned above. It did not take long for him to become involved with the various conspiracy groups intent on overthrowing the Nazi grip of government, and because of his involvement with such groups was duly executed.

These diaries are like searchlights shining into the blackened past from different angles, digging up the events, the ongoing gossip, the feelings and emotions of the day. They are a significant aspect of Oral History, not least by making it interesting as they were written at the time by people who were there.

Chapter Four also relates directly to Oral History as it draws attention to notes or recordings taken at the time. In any court of law such evidence is regarded as critical for defining the truth of what happened, and the intentions and acts of those involved in any form of crime. This is why even in the civilian world police try to place listening bugs or a secret undercover officer within the area of investigation, and they keep detailed notes from interviews. For gathering information as to what key figures were thinking or had thought at the military level in the past, it is still deemed historically essential to find a way of understanding their way of thinking, namely their mindsets. Bugging the private conversations of senior German officers was a clever way of gaining the necessary insights, because although they were prisoners and many knew the war was lost, such information exposed their past as well as their present views, from which the 'wheat and chaff' could be separated, but more to the point it offered many insights into the political and military minds of leading German officers. They were genuine leads for the listeners as it was clear that despite natural suspicion by some prisoners the bugging devices were cleverly concealed making the conversations seem totally confidential.

When the major culprits were at Nuremberg, they were professionally interrogated, and observed all the time, often even when they were asleep as the guards were concerned about possible suicide attempts. The prisoners would have been very alert to their predicament and the likely sentence of death or a long imprisonment. As such many if not most of them were seemingly changed characters, pretending they did not know about the mass slaughter of Jews and other massacres, relying on the defence of good men doing their national duties by obeying orders, and sometimes claiming that they had been misled. What made Goldensohn's book so fascinating was that he was attending them as a medic, and as a firm but seemingly easy person many of them related to him with ease, even pleased to see him. But he was a professional medical man of the mind and knew how to talk with them, and his observations are sharp and to the point. In some ways this writer wished there had been no executions, as it would have been more useful for them to spend the rest of their natural lives being explored by men like Goldensohn and his medical colleagues to try and understand not just what made them tick, but the nature of the human environment which drives men like these prisoners to such disastrous and immoral behaviour. However, and more to the point, these medical conversations are enlightening in many ways and reflect sound Oral History.

It is easy to obtain or view the written recordings of the postwar trials, especially the major ones of the leading characters at Nuremberg. On reading these papers it is like stepping back in time and being in the courtroom. It is almost possible for the reader to feel they met these major figures. Whether it was the self-pitying and 'weak-kneed' Ribbentrop, or the 'bully-boy' Göring, who during his courtroom interrogation was still clever enough to cause the prosecution some embarrassment. It is a sharp reminder of Oral History that such people may have been long dead by rope or time, but their characteristics and behaviour patterns can still be found in leading figures of today.

Chapter Five moved into the area of reminiscent history, called by some the heritage of memory. Parts of this aspect can be found in Chapter One where some published books are a mixture of both oral history and memory. This chapter looks at a few autobiographies selected not just because of their reality and checking other sources, but often because the author is felt to be honest, some admitting to committing crimes, others of being scared stiff, and it is known that some kept notes from the times of action. As mentioned earlier in the text this writer can recall talking to old First World War trench soldiers in a British Legion Home in Aylesford Kent some fifty years after 1918. There was never any reason to doubt what they said, and the impression gained was that the horror and misery of the trenches did not need exaggeration and their memories did not need changing, it was for many of them as if it happened yesterday.

Books based on memory-recall can be good and interesting to read, so long as they feel authentic, the historical data can often be checked and looking for clues such as the reader's surprise that the writer included some parts of his own behaviour and reactions. Memory recall can be enlightening, but as with some Oral History some components need at times double checking. One of the clues for authenticity is when the reader might at times thinks it surprising the writer included 'that detail'. Some admitted to being scared to death, having breakdowns, feeling incompetent, others to theft and one to being in a military prison. Another British soldier was ashamed of being British. The German and British fighter pilots both commented on the disruptive and emotional feeling of waiting for the call to fly into combat, the fear of waiting, with the German pilot referring to it as the 'channel sickness'. The three selected frontline soldiers often mention cases of theft, some of drink, and some of women. In common they offer their experiences of their various battles and conflicts, problems with officers and one another. This is more interesting than studying the maps and the views of senior commanders, because these frontline men were seeing it from personal experience.

The best and honest autobiographical accounts are a valid time-capsule as they take us back to the emotions and feelings of the day, which are often conveyed more accurately and in a meaningful way to the next generation. There is no denying that they make for more interesting reading than working one's way through old notes. A sound autobiography manages to take us back in the past to remind us how we may have felt in those days, because history is not just about facts and figures, it about humankind's thinking, feelings, and emotions.

There is some 'appeal' in reading diaries, personal letters, honest reflections, and notes of years gone by, and it is their immediacy and intimacy, the unique sense of being there and sharing or involved in that time which gives more than a mere flavour but offers a personal insight. This sense of 'being there' comes through strongly with some autobiographies and in a more appealing way for the general reader. Oral history in its various shapes, from direct oral evidence to reflective accounts makes history interesting and brings home its importance to humankind.

Notes

Chapter 1

1. See Howarth, Ken, *Oral History: A Handbook* (Stroud: Sutton Publishing, 1999).
2. Liddle, Peter, *Captured Memories 1930–1945: Across the Threshold of War* (Barnsley: Pen & Sword, 2011).
3. Holmes, Richard, *The World at War: The Landmark Oral History from the Previously Unpublished Archives* (London: Ebury Press, 2007).
4. Ibid., p.168.
5. Ibid., p.595.
6. Ibid., p.186.
7. Ibid., p.43 and p.314.
8. Ibid., p.418 and p.420.
9. Levine, Joshua, *Forgotten Voices of the Blitz and the Battle for Britain* (London: Ebury Press, 2006).
10. Ibid., pp.113–18.
11. Ibid., p.328.
12. Ibid.
13. Owen, James and Walters, Guy (Eds), *The Voice of War: The Second World War Told by Those Who Fought It* (London: Viking (Penguin), 2004).
14. Ibid., p.249.
15. Ibid., p.257.
16. Ibid., p.310.
17. Ibid., p.573.
18. Arthur, Max, *Forgotten Voices of The Great War* (London: Ebury Press, 2002).
19. Ibid., p.140.
20. Ibid., p.243.
21. Arthur, Max, *Last Post* (London: Weidenfeld & Nicolson, 2005).
22. Arthur, Max, *Lost Voices of the Royal Navy* (London: Hodder, 1997).
23. Ibid., p.34.
24. Ibid., p.56.
25. Ibid., p.105.
26. Ibid., p.147.
27. Arthur, Max, *Lost Voices of the Royal Air Force* (London: Hodder, 1993).
28. Ibid., p.255.
29. Ibid., p.262.
30. Ibid., pp.283ff.
31. Carruthers, Bob, *Voices from the Luftwaffe* (Barnsley: Pen & Sword, 2011).

32. Ibid., p.71.
33. Elborough, Travis, *Our History of the 20th Century: As Told in Diaries, Journals and Letters* (London: Michael O'Mara Books, 2017).

Chapter 2

1. Himmler, Katrin and Wildt, Michael (Eds), *The Private Heinrich Himmler: Letters of a Mass Murderer* (New York: St Martin's Press, 2016).
2. Toland, John, *The Last 100 Days* (New York: The Modern Library, 1996), p.133.
3. Quoted in Longerich, Peter, *Heinrich Himmler* (Oxford: OUP, 2012), p.204.
4. Ibid., p.551.
5. Ibid., p.720.
6. Kershaw, Ian, *The End: The Defiance and Destruction of Hitler's Germany, 1944–1945* (London: Penguin Books, 2012), pp.229, 330 and 336.
7. Edited by Katrin Himmler and Michael Wildt, *The Private Heinrich Himmler: Letters of a Mass Murderer* (New York: St Martin's Press, 2016), p.170.
8. Roberts, Stephen H., *The House that Hitler Built* (London: Methuen, 1938), pp.89–90.
9. Chervatin, Dirk, *Eastern Front: 500 Letters from War* (EK-2 Publishing, 2022).
10. Ibid., p.6
11. Liddell-Hart, B.H. (Ed. with others), *The Rommel Papers* (London: Da Capo Press, 1953).
12. Ibid., p.7.
13. Ibid., p.34.
14. Ibid., p.53.
15. Ibid., p.57.
16. Ibid., p.103.
17. Ibid., p.111.
18. Ibid., p.124.
19. Ibid., p.131.
20. Ibid., p.174.
21. Ibid., p.176.
22. Ibid., p.183.
23. Ibid., p.139.
24. Ibid., p.151.
25. Ibid., p.160.
26. Ibid., p.170.
27. Ibid., p.224.
28. Ibid., p.255.
29. Ibid., p.263.
30. Ibid., p.292.
31. Ibid., p.388.
32. Ibid., p.380.
33. Schraepler, Hans-Albrecht (Ed.), *At Rommel's Side: The Lost Letters of Hans-Joachim Schraepler* (Barnsley, Frontline Books, 2009).
34. Ibid., p.173.
35. Ibid., p.52.
36. Ibid., p.93.

37. Ibid., p.53.

38. Ibid.

39. Ibid., p.56.

40. Ibid., p.64.

41. Ibid., p.72.

42. Ibid., p.86.

43. Ibid., p.63.

44. Ibid., p.167.

45. Ibid., p.58.

46. Ibid., p.77.

47. Ibid., p.99.

48. Ibid., p.127.

49. Ibid., p.78.

50. Ibid., p.81.

51. Ibid., p.94.

52. Ibid., p.154.

53. Ibid., p.94

54. Ibid., p.61.

55. Ibid., p.68.

56. Ibid., p.97.

57. Ibid., p.98, p.100 and p.111.

58. Ibid., p.125.

59. Ibid., p.161.

60. D'Este, Carlo, *Patton: A Genius for War* (New York: Harper Perennial, 1996), p.433.

61. Blumenson, Martin, *The Patton Papers 1940–1945* (New York: Da Capo Press, 1996), p.274.

62. See Atkinson, Rick, *The Day of the Battle* (London: Abacus, 2013), p.43.

63. Porch, Douglas, *Hitler's Mediterranean Gamble* (London: Cassell, 2005), p.448.

64. Weinberg, Gerhard L., *A World at Arms* (Cambridge: CUP, 1994), p.918.

65. Blumenson, Martin, *The Patton Papers 1940–1945*, p.288.

66. Atkinson, Rick, *The Day of the Battle*, p.148.

67. See D'Este, Carlo, *Patton: A Genius for War*, p.496.

68. Atkinson, Rick, *The Day of the Battle*, p.44.

69. Blumenson, Martin, *The Patton Papers 1940–1945*, p.175.

70. Axelrod, Alan, *Patton: A Biography* (London: Palgrave Macmillan, 2006), p.2.

71. Blumenson, Martin, *The Patton Papers 1940–1945*.

72. Ibid., p.x.

73. Ibid., p.27.

74. Ibid., p.97.

75. Ibid., p.111.

76. Ibid., p.116.

77. Ibid., p.130.

78. Ibid., p.133.

79. Ibid., p.141.

80. Davison, Peter (Ed.), *The Orwell Diaries* (London: Penguin Books, 2010).

81. Davison, Peter (Ed.), *A Life in Letters* (London: Penguin Books, 2011).

82. Ibid., p.173.
83. Ibid., p.174.
84. Ibid., p.179.
85. Ibid., p.203.
86. Ibid., p.204.
87. Ibid., p.208.

Chapter 3

1. Colville, John, *The Fringes of Power* (London: Hodder & Stoughton, 1985), p.256.
2. Ibid., p.326.
3. Alanbrooke, Field Marshal Lord, *War Diaries 1939–1945* (London: Weidenfeld & Nicolson, 2001).
4. *The Times*, 18 June 1963 Obituary.
5. Quoted in Roberts, Andrew, *Masters and Commanders: The Military Geniuses Who Led the West to Victory in WWII* (London: Penguin Books, 2009), p.91.
6. *Shrapnel* was his codename initially.
7. Alanbrooke, Field Marshal Lord, *War Diaries 1939–1945* (London: Weidenfeld & Nicolson, 2001), p.191.
8. Bradley Omar, *A General's Life* (London: Sidgwick & Jackson, 1983) p.159.
9. Roberts, Andrew, *Masters and Commanders* (London: Penguin Books, 2009), p.277.
10. Kennedy, Major-General Sir John, *The Business of War* (London: Hutchinson, 1957), p.275.
11. See Roberts, Andrew, *Masters and Commanders*, p.42.
12. Colville, John, *The Churchillians* (London: Weidenfeld & Nicolson, 1981), p.143.
13. Farrell, Nicholas, *Mussolini: A New Life* (London: Sharpe Books, 2018), p.322.
14. Eden, Anthony, The Rt. Hon. The Earl of Avon, *The Eden Memoirs: Facing the Dictators* (London: Cassell, 1962), pp.214–15.
15. Smyth, Howard McGaw, *Secrets of the Fascist Era* (Illinois: Southern Illinois University Press, 1975), p.24.
16. Ciano, Galeazzo, Muggeridge, M. (Ed.), *Ciano's Diary 1939–1943* (London: William Heinemann, 1947), p.88.
17. Schellenberg, Walter, *Schellenberg* (London: Mayflower, 1965), p.16.
18. Ciano, Galeazzo, De Felice, Renzo (Ed.), *Ciano's Diary 1937–1943* (London: Phoenix Press, 2002), p.318.
19. Ibid., p.341.
20. Ciano, Galeazzo, Muggeridge, M. (Ed.), *Ciano's Diary 1939–1943*, p.258.
21. See Sangster, Andrew, *The Futile Pursuit of Power: Why Mussolini Executed his Son-in Law* (Dunbeath, Caithness: Whittles, 2023)
22. Klemperer, Victor (Translated by Martin Chalmers), *I Shall Bear Witness: The Diaries of Victor Klemperer 1933–41* (Weidenfeld & Nicolson, London, 1998); Klemperer, Victor (Translated by Martin Chalmers), *The Bitter End, The Diaries of Victor Klemperer 1942-1945* (Weidenfeld & Nicolson, London, 1999); Klemperer, Victor (Translated by Martin Chalmers), *The Lesser Evil, The Diaries of Victor Klemperer 1945–59* (Phoenix an imprint of Orion Books, London, 2004).
23. Sangster, Andrew, *The Unfolding Agony of Oppression* (Ethics International Press, 2023).

24. See Reimann, Viktor, *Joseph Goebbels: The Man Who Created Hitler* (London: Sphere Books Ltd, 1979), p.2.
25. Heiber, Helmut, *Goebbels* (New York: Hawthorn Books, 1972), p.5.
26. *The Goebbels Diaries 1939–41* (Translated by Taylor, Fred) (London: Hamish Hamilton, 1982), pp.19–20.
27. Ibid., p.22.
28. Ibid., p.75.
29. Ibid., p.21.
30. Ibid., p.21.
31. Ibid., p.25.
32. Ibid., p.66.
33. Ibid., p.67.
34. Ibid., p.36.
35. Ibid., p.38.
36. Ibid., p.46.
37. Ibid., p.60.
38. Ibid., p.56.
39. Ibid., p.77.
40. Vassiltchikov, Marie 'Missie', *The Berlin Diaries 1940–1945* (London: Pimlico, 1999).
41. Ibid., p.13.
42. Ibid., p.269.
43. Ibid., p36.
44. Ibid., p.22.
45. Ibid., p.45
46. Ibid., p.87.
47. Ibid., p.189.
48. Ibid., p.4.
49. Ibid., p.27.
50. Ibid., p.10.
51. Ibid., p.2.
52. Ibid., pp.81–2.
53. Ibid., p.50
54. Ibid., p.17.
55. Ibid., p.148.
56. Ibid., p.151.
57. Ibid., p.178.
58. Ibid., p.185.
59. Ibid., p.200.
60. Ibid., p.207.
61. Ibid., p.229.
62. Müller-Hill, Otto, *The True German: The Diary of a World War II Military Judge* (London: Palgrave, 2013).
63. Ibid., p.170.
64. Ibid., p.7.
65. Ibid., p.151.

66. Ibid., p.27.
67. Ibid., p.40.
68. Ibid., p.173.
69. Ibid., p.32.
70. Ibid., p.7.
71. Ibid., p.38.
72. Ibid., p.48.
73. Ibid., p.11.
74. Ibid., pp.84–5.
75. Ibid., p.132.
76. Ibid., p.135
77. Ibid., p.136.
78. Ibid., p.21.
79. Ibid., p.52.
80. Ibid., p.68.
81. Ibid., p.78.
82. Ibid., p.175.
83. Ibid., p.97.
84. Ibid., p.101.
85. Ibid., p.102.
86. Ibid., p.110.
87. Ibid., p.107.
88. Ibid., p.29.
89. Ibid., p.92.
90. Ibid., p.46.
91. Ibid., p.104.
92. Ibid., p.165.
93. Hart-Davis, Duff (Ed.) *King's Counsellor: Abdication and War: the Diaries of Sir Alan Lascelles* (London: Weidenfeld & Nicolson, 2006).
94. Ibid., p.10.
95. Ibid., p.95.
96. Ibid., p.136.
97. Ibid., p.176.
98. Ibid., p.15.
99. Ibid., p.17.
100. Ibid., p.35.
101. Ibid., p.43.
102. Ibid., p.56.
103. Ibid., p.132.
104. Ibid., p.62.
105. Ibid., p.103.
106. Ibid., p.126.
107. Ibid., p.150.
108. Ibid., p.171.
109. Ibid., p.224.
110. Ibid., p.225.

111. Ibid., p.229.
112. Ibid., p.233.
113. Kennedy, Major-General Sir John, *The Business of War* (London: Hutchinson, 1957), p.268.
114. Hart-Davis, Duff (Ed.) *King's Counsellor*, p.73.
115. Colville, John, *The Fringes of Power: Downing Street Diaries 1939–1955* (London: Hodder & Stoughton, 1985), p.29.
116. Ibid., p.34.
117. Ibid., p.35.
118. Ibid., p.43.
119. Ibid., p.152.
120. Ibid., p.284.
121. Ibid., p.45.
122. Ibid., p.182.
123. Ibid., p.235.
124. Ibid., p.46.
125. Ibid., p.50.
126. Ibid., p.108.
127. Ibid., p.112.
128. Ibid., p.51.
129. Ibid., p.71.
130. Ibid., p.126.
131. Ibid., p.135.
132. Ibid., p.136.
133. Ibid., p.148.
134. Ibid., p.488.
135. Ibid., p.518.
136. Ibid., p.551.
137. *The Times*, Obituary Page, 19 November 1987.
138. Sangster, Andrew, *The Futile Pursuit of Power*, p.36.
139. Hassell, Ulrich von, *The Ulrich von Hassell Diaries, 1938–1944* (London: Frontline Books, 2011).
140. Ibid., p.9.
141. Ibid., p.10.
142. Ibid., p.31.
143. Ibid., p.35.
144. Ibid., p.43.
145. Ibid., p.34.
146. Ibid., p.128.
147. Ibid.
148. Ibid., p.157.

Chapter 4

1. Neitzel, Sönke (Ed.), *Tapping Hitler's Generals: Transcripts of Secret Conversations, 1942–45* (Barnsley: Pen & Sword Books, 2007).
2. Sangster, Andrew, *From Stalingrad to Italy – Von Senger's War: The German General Who Defied Hitler* (Barnsley: Pen & Sword, 2025), p.126.

3. Neitzel, Sönke (Ed.), *Tapping Hitler's Generals: Transcripts of Secret Conversations, 1942–45* (Barnsley: Pen & Sword Books, 2007), p.65.
4. Ibid., p.79.
5. Ibid., pp.81–2.
6. Ibid., p.83.
7. Ibid., p.86.
8. Ibid., p.94.
9. Ibid., p.130.
10. Ibid., p.145.
11. Ibid., p.157.
12. Ibid., p.170.
13. Gellately, Robert (Ed.), *The Nuremberg Interviews* (London: Pimlico, 2007).
14. Ibid., p.12.
15. Ibid., p.13.
16. Ibid., p.101.
17. Ibid., p.107.
18. Ibid., p.121.
19. Ibid., p.113.
20. Ibid., p.114.
21. Ibid., p.127.
22. Ibid., p.130.
23. Ibid., p.183.
24. Ibid., p.184.
25. Ibid., p.185.
26. Ibid.
27. Ibid., p.189.
28. Ibid., p.252.
29. Ibid., p.253.
30. Ibid., p.262.
31. *The Trial of German Major War Criminals*, Part 5 (H.M. Attorney-General by his Majesty's Stationery Office, London, 1946)
32. See Ibid., p.199.
33. Ibid., p.182.
34. Ibid., p.183.
35. Ibid., p.185.
36. Ibid., p.193.
37. Nuremberg Trial Papers, 17 January 1946.

Chapter 5

1. Wellum, Geoffrey, *First Light* (London: Penguin Books, 2003), p.xiv.
2. Ibid., p.126 and p.263.
3. Ibid., p.43.
4. Ibid., p.112.
5. Ibid., p.153.
6. Ibid., p.301.
7. Ibid., p.22.

8. Ibid., p.169.

9. Steinhilper, Ulrich, and Osborne, Peter, *Spitfire on My Tail: A View from the Other Side* (Bromley: Independent Books, 1989).

10. Ibid., p.29.

11. Ibid., p.35.

12. Ibid., p.83.

13. Ibid., p.97.

14. Ibid., p.209.

15. Ibid., p.195.

16. Ibid., p.245.

17. Ibid., p.276.

18. Ibid., p.277.

19. Ibid., p.285.

20. Ibid, p.292.

21. Cambridge, Reginald, *It's a Long Way to Tooting Broadway* (CreateSpace Independent Publishing, 2015).

22. Ibid., p.2.

23. Ibid., p.28.

24. Ibid., p.39.

25. Ibid., p.121.

26. *The Times*, 5 September 2005.

27. Bowlby, Alex, *The Recollections of Rifleman Bowlby* (London: Cassell & Co, 2002), Introduction.

28. Ibid., p.209.

29. Ibid., p.88.

30. Ibid., p.82.

31. See Ibid., p.91.

32. Ibid., p.15.

33. Ibid., p.16.

34. Ibid., p.20.

35. Ibid., p.55.

36. Ibid., p.21.

37. Ibid., p.118.

38. Ibid., p.50.

39. Ibid., p.71.

40. Ibid., p.74.

41. Ibid., p.181.

42. Ibid., p.25.

43. Ibid., p.26.

44. Ibid., p.74.

45. Ibid., p.178.

46. Gregg, Victor (Assisted by Stroud, Rick), *Rifleman: A Front-Line Life from Alamein and Dresden to the Fall of the Berlin Wall* (London: Bloomsbury, 2011).

47. Ibid., p.23.

48. Ibid., p.44.

49. Ibid., p.59.

50. Ibid., p.61.
51. Ibid., p.96 and p.100.
52. Ibid., p.69.
53. Ibid., p.73.
54. Ibid., p.82.
55. Ibid., p.91.
56. Ibid., p.115.
57. Ibid., p.118.
58. Ibid., p.176.
59. Ibid., p.179.
60. Ibid., p.xi.

Bibliography

Alanbrooke, Field Marshal Lord, *War Diaries 1939–1945* (London: Weidenfeld & Nicolson, 2001)

Arthur, Max, *Forgotten Voices of The Great War* (London: Ebury Press, 2002)

——, *Lost Voices of the Royal Navy* (London: Hodder, 1997)

——, *Lost Voices of the Royal Air Force* (London: Hodder, 1993)

——, *Last Post: The Final Word from our First World War Soldiers* (London: Weidenfeld & Nicolson, 2005)

Atkinson, Rick, *The Day of the Battle: The War in Sicily and Italy 1943–1944* (London: Abacus, 2013)

Axelrod, Alan, *Patton: A Biography* (London: Palgrave Macmillan, 2006)

Blumenson, Martin, *The Patton Papers 1940–1945* (New York: Da Capo Press, 1996)

Bowlby, Alex, *The Recollections of Rifleman Bowlby* (London: Cassell & Co, 2002)

Bradley, Omar, *A General's Life* (London: Sidgwick & Jackson, 1983)

Cambridge, Reginald, *It's a Long Way to Tooting Broadway* (CreateSpace Independent Publishing, 2015)

Chervatin, Dirk, *Eastern Front: 500 Letters from War* (EK-2 Publishing, 2022)

Ciano, Galeazzo, Muggeridge, M. (Ed.), *Ciano's Diary 1939–1943* (London: William Heinemann, 1947)

Ciano, Galeazzo, De Felice, Renzo (Ed.), *Ciano's Diary 1937–1943* (London: Phoenix Press, 2002)

Colville, John, *The Churchillians* (London: Weidenfeld & Nicolson, 1981)

——, *The Fringes of Power: Downing Street Diaries 1939–1955* (London: Hodder & Stoughton, 1985)

Carruthers, Bob, *Voices from the Luftwaffe* (Barnsley: Pen & Sword, 2011)

D'Este, Carlo, *Patton: A Genius for War* (New York: Harper Perennial, 1996)

Eden, Anthony, The Rt. Hon. The Earl of Avon, *The Eden Memoirs: Facing the Dictators* (London: Cassell, 1962)

Elborough, Travis, *Our History of the 20th Century: As Told in Diaries, Journals and Letters* (London: Michael O'Mara Books, 2017)

Farrell, Nicholas, *Mussolini: A New Life* (London: Sharpe Books, 2018)

Goebbels, Joseph (Translated by Taylor, Fred), *The Goebbels Diaries, 1939–1941* (London: Hamish Hamilton, 1982)

Gregg, Victor (Assisted by Stroud, Rick), *Rifleman: A Front-line Life from Alamein and Dresden to the Fall of the Berlin Wall* (London: Bloomsbury, 2011)

Hassell, Ulrich von, *The Ulrich von Hassell Diaries, 1938–1944* (London: Frontline Books, 2011)

Heiber, Helmut, *Goebbels* (New York: Hawthorn Books, 1972)

Himmler, Katrin and Wildt, Michael (Eds), *The Private Heinrich Himmler: Letters of a Mass Murderer* (New York: St Martin's Press, 2016)

Holmes, Richard, *The World at War: The Landmark Oral History from the Previously Unpublished Archives* (London: Ebury Press, 2007)

Howarth, Ken, *Oral History: A Handbook* (Stroud: Sutton Publishing, 1999)

Kennedy, Major-General Sir John, *The Business of War* (London: Hutchinson, 1957)

Kershaw, Ian, *The End: The Defiance and Destruction of Hitler's Germany, 1944–1945* (London: Penguin Books, 2012)

Klemperer, Victor (Translated by Martin Chalmers), *I Shall Bear Witness: The Diaries of Victor Klemperer 1933–41* (Weidenfeld & Nicolson, London, 1998)

——, *To The Bitter End, The Diaries of Victor Klemperer 1942–45* (Weidenfeld & Nicolson, London, 1999)

——, *The Lesser Evil, The Diaries of Victor Klemperer 1945–59* (Phoenix an imprint of Orion Books, London, 2004)

Lascelles, Sir Alan, Hart-Davis, Duff (Ed.), *King's Counsellor: Abdication and War: The Diaries of Sir Alan Lascelles* (London: Weidenfeld & Nicholson, 2006)

Levine, Joshua, *Forgotten Voices of the Blitz and the Battle for Britain* (London: Ebury Press, 2006)

Liddell-Hart, B.H. (Ed. with others), *The Rommel Papers* (London: Da Capo Press, 1953)

Liddle, Peter, *Captured Memories 1930–1945: Across the Threshold of War* (Barnsley: Pen & Sword, 2011)

Longerich, Peter, *Heinrich Himmler* (Oxford: OUP, 2012)

Macmillan, Harold, *War Diaries: The Mediterranean 1943–1945* (London: Macmillan, 1984)

Manvell, Roger and Fraenkel, Heinrich, *Heinrich Himmler: The Sinister Life of the Head of the SS and Gestapo* (London: Skyhorse Publishing, 2007)

Müller-Hill, Otto, *The True German: The Diary of a World War II Military Judge* (London: Palgrave, 2013)

Neitzel, Sönke (Ed.), *Tapping Hitler's Generals: Transcripts of Secret Conversations, 1942–45* (Barnsley: Pen & Sword Books, 2007)

Owen, James and Walters, Guy (Eds), *The Voice of War: The Second World War Told by Those Who Fought It* (London: Viking (Penguin) 2004)

Porch, Douglas, *Hitler's Mediterranean Gamble: The North African and the Mediterranean Campaigns in World War II* (London: Cassell, 2005)

Reimann, Viktor, *Joseph Goebbels: The Man Who Created Hitler* (London: Sphere Books Ltd, 1979)

Roberts, Andrew, *Masters and Commanders: The Military Geniuses Who Led the West to Victory in WWII* (London: Penguin Books, 2009)

Roberts, Stephen H., *The House that Hitler Built* (London: Methuen, 1938)

Sangster, Andrew, *The Futile Pursuit of Power: Why Mussolini Executed his Son-in-Law* (Dunbeath, Caithness: Whittles, 2023)

——, *The Unfolding Agony of Oppression* (Ethics International Press, 2023)

——, *From Stalingrad to Italy – Von Senger's War: The German General Who Defied Hitler* (Barnsley: Pen & Sword, 2025)

Schellenberg, Walter, *Schellenberg* (London: Mayflower, 1965)

Schraepler, Hans-Albrecht (Ed.), *At Rommel's Side: The Lost Letters of Hans-Joachim Schraepler* (Barnsley, Frontline Books, 2009)

Smyth, Howard McGaw, *Secrets of the Fascist Era* (Illinois: Southern Illinois University Press, 1975)

Steinhilper, Ulrich, and Osborne, Peter, *Spitfire on My Tail: A View from the Other Side* (Bromley: Independent Books, 1989)

Toland, John, *The Last 100 Days: The Tumultuous and Controversial Story of the Final Days of World War II in Europe* (New York: The Modern Library, 1996)

Weinberg, Gerhard L., *A World at Arms: A Global History of World War II* (Cambridge: CUP, 1994)

Wellum, Geoffrey, *First Light* (London: Penguin Books, 2003)

Primary Sources

Nuremberg Trial Papers, 17 January 1946

The Trial of German Major War Criminals, Part 5 (H.M. Attorney-General by his Majesty's Stationery Office, London, 1946)

The Times, 18 June 1963 Obituary

The Times, 19 November 1987 Obituary

The Times, 5 September 2005

Index

Dear Reader,

We hope you have enjoyed this book, but why not share your views on social media? You can also follow our pages to see more about our other products: facebook.com/penandswordbooks or follow us on X @penswordbooks

You can also view our products at www.pen-and-sword.co.uk (UK and ROW) or www.penandswordbooks.com (North America).

To keep up to date with our latest releases and online catalogues, please sign up to our newsletter at: www.pen-and-sword.co.uk/newsletter

If you would like a printed catalogue with our latest books, then please email: enquiries@pen-and-sword.co.uk or telephone: 01226 734555 (UK and ROW) or email: uspen-and-sword@casematepublishers.com or telephone: (610) 853-9131 (North America).

We respect your privacy and we will only use personal information to send you information about our products.

Thank you!